"Walton and Longman, two seasoned commentators on Job, argue that readers should redirect their efforts from seeking reasons in its pages for human suffering to instead recognizing the lesson to trust in a sovereign God with the incongruities of life. The pious may not understand their painful lot, but assurance and rest come in accepting the wisdom of the Almighty. Thoughtful and accessible, this is a welcome addition to the How To Read series."
M. Daniel Carroll R., Distinguished Professor of Old Testament, Denver Seminary

"This readable volume questions many traditional answers to Job. It also provides important perspectives on the book's interpretation. It is an excellent starting point for the reader of this great literary masterpiece of the Bible."
Richard S. Hess, Earl S. Kalland Professor of Old Testament and Semitic Languages

"The book of Job is a weighty read at just about every level, from its language to its theology. Walton and Longman's *How to Read Job* is a helpful training manual for the task. Their treatment of the discrete interpretive issues is clear and concise. Taken as a whole, their individual discussions guide the reader of Job from an understanding of the book in its ancient context to its Christian application as Scripture. Walton and Longman take unequivocal interpretive stances on various of the book's conundrums and they provide questions to prompt the reader to further reflection. The best feature of this short primer on the book of Job is that it draws one to read the book of Job itself rather than substituting lengthy commentary for the biblical text. Students, pastors and laity can all benefit from this delightfully accessible invitation to the book of Job."
John A. Cook, Asbury Theological Seminary

T0346595

HOW TO READ
JOB

JOHN H. WALTON
TREMPER LONGMAN III

IVP Academic

An imprint of InterVarsity Press
Downers Grove, Illinois

InterVarsity Press
P.O. Box 1400, Downers Grove, IL 60515-1426
ivpress.com
email@ivpress.com

©2015 by John H. Walton and Tremper Longman III

All rights reserved. No part of this book may be reproduced in any form without written permission from InterVarsity Press.

InterVarsity Press® is the book-publishing division of InterVarsity Christian Fellowship/USA®, a movement of students and faculty active on campus at hundreds of universities, colleges and schools of nursing in the United States of America, and a member movement of the International Fellowship of Evangelical Students. For information about local and regional activities, visit intervarsity.org.

All Scripture quotations, unless otherwise indicated, are taken from THE HOLY BIBLE, NEW INTERNATIONAL VERSION®, NIV® Copyright © 1973, 1978, 1984, 2011 by Biblica, Inc.™ Used by permission. All rights reserved worldwide.

Cover design: Cindy Kiple
Interior design: Beth McGill
Images: Roberta Polfus

ISBN 978-0-8308-4089-2 (print)
ISBN 978-0-8308-9907-4 (digital)

Printed in the United States of America ♾

 As a member of the Green Press Initiative, InterVarsity Press is committed to protecting the environment and to the responsible use of natural resources. To learn more, visit greenpressinitiative.org.

Library of Congress Cataloging-in-Publication Data

Walton, John H., 1952-
  How to read Job / John H. Walton and Tremper Longman III.
      pages cm
  Includes bibliographical references and index.
  ISBN 978-0-8308-4089-2 (pbk. : alk. paper)
  1. Bible. Job--Criticism, interpretation, etc. 2. Bible. Job--Hermeneutics. I. Title.
  BS1415.52.W35 2015
  223'.106--dc23

                                                                                    2015027310

P	20	19	18	17	16	15	14	13	12	11	10	9	8	7	6	5	4	3	2	1
Y	32	31	30	29	28	27	26	25	24	23	22	21	20	19	18	17	16	15			

To Kim Walton and Alice Longman

CONTENTS

ACKNOWLEDGMENTS

I (John Walton) would like to give special thanks to Jonathan Walton, Kimberly Carlton and Aubrey Buster for reading the manuscript and offering their ever stimulating and helpful insights to improve it in untold ways.

As always, I (Tremper Longman) want to express my gratitude to my wife, Alice, for her support and encouragement.

We both want to thank Dan Reid for his friendship as well as his editorial guidance on this project. We also thank the staff at IVP Academic, including Ben McCoy, Rebecca Carhart, Maureen Tobey, Ashley Davila and Jeanna Wiggins for their care in bringing this book to publication.

1

READING JOB
AS LITERATURE

■   ■   ■

ONE

WHAT IS THE
BOOK OF JOB ABOUT?

It is not uncommon for people to turn to the book of Job when they encounter suffering, but all too often they find the book unsatisfying. They think that the book will explain why they or their loved ones are suffering or why there is so much suffering in the world. They have the impression that the book is about Job and that he is going to provide a model for how they should respond in times of suffering. They expect to learn why God acts the way that he does—why he allows or even causes righteous people to suffer. It is no wonder, then, that they find the book inadequate; their expectations are misguided. We need to begin, then, with some adjustments to our expectations. First of all, Job has trials, but he is not on trial. We will propose that God's policies are on trial. Second, the book of Job is not primarily about Job; it is primarily about God. Third, if this is so, the book is more about the reasons for righteousness than about the reasons for suffering. Finally, the topic of wisdom plays a central role in the book. Indeed, Job's suffering leads to a heated debate as to who has the wisdom that will help the characters diagnose and prescribe a remedy for Job's problems. Here we will see that, though all the human characters claim that they are wise, it is only God who is wise. Let's look at these in more detail.

JOB HAS TRIALS, BUT HE IS NOT ON TRIAL

Job is declared innocent and righteous from the beginning of the book and throughout it, so there is no doubt that he *is* righteous. The question is whether he will retain his integrity. His integrity is defined by whether he will keep his focus on his righteousness or pursue a strategy to recover the benefits of a righteous life. If his focus is his benefits, it will show that the challenge posed against him is a correct assessment: he does not serve God for nothing (Job 1:9).

While Job clearly has trials, he and his friends more importantly believe that he is *on trial*. Job considers himself to be the defendant in a criminal case. In his mind, he has been treated as a wicked person and is now trying to defend himself. His defense follows the strategy of trying to reposition himself as a plaintiff in a civil case. Because he perceives this to be the scenario, he demands a hearing so that he can lodge a complaint against the one who has falsely accused him. In reality, however, his role is to serve as the star witness for the defense, because it is God's policies that are on trial.

This view of the book is substantiated when we see the issue that is raised for discussion in Job 1:9. The challenge does not suggest that Job is not truly righteous—in fact, his righteousness is accepted as a premise. The challenge concerns Job's motivations for being righteous: "Does Job fear God for nothing?" Such a challenge ultimately questions God's policy of blessing righteous people. The contention is that if God makes it a policy to bring prosperity as a reward for righteousness, true righteousness will be subverted because people will act righteously in order to gain benefits. God, therefore, by his very policy, is creating mercenaries of a sort—people who will do anything to get ahead.

The fundamental issue at question in the book of Job is whether it is good policy for God to bless the righteous by bringing them prosperity (wealth and health). The challenger (identified as *satan*; see chap. 6 for explanation) argues that it is not good policy and suggests that the mettle of Job's righteousness, if tested by the removal of all his benefits, will prove lacking. That would demonstrate that his righteousness was founded only in his own search for gain and was never true righteousness at all. However, this scrutiny of Job's motives is only a means to an end. The main question concerns how God runs the world.

ABOUT GOD, NOT ABOUT JOB

Certainly Job gets more "airtime" than God in the book. In the end, however, it is not important whether we understand Job better. His character does not provide a guide for how we ought to think or act. Much of what Job thinks and says is at least partially wrong. How Job responds is ultimately important so that we can consider how God runs the world and whether there can be such a thing as disinterested righteousness (serving God for nothing).

The focus on God becomes even clearer when we see the second piece of the challenge. The first challenge suggests that God's policy of blessing righteous people is flawed because it seems to buy people's loyalty and righteousness. The second piece of the challenge falls into place when Job begins to suffer. As he makes his speeches and launches his demands to God for a hearing, we learn that Job also has a problem with God's policies: he considers it bad policy that God allows righteous people to suffer. In short, he thinks that God is unjust.

These two challenges set up the focus of the book as it pertains to God's policies in the world: it is not good policy for righteous people to prosper (for that undermines the development of true righteousness by providing an ulterior motive). In tension with that, it is not good policy for righteous people to suffer (they are the good people, the ones who are on God's side). So what is God to do?

Not only do these two challenges shape the book, but they also inevitably lead to deeper questions: Is it really God's policy to bless the righteous and bring suffering only to the wicked? If so, why does experience so often suggest that this is not true? How does God run the world? Can we affirm that his policies are the best policies? Recognizing that these are the questions being addressed, we can now see how it is that this book is primarily about God. Job is the test case for considering how God runs the world and how we should think about God when life goes haywire.

ABOUT THE REASONS FOR RIGHTEOUSNESS, NOT THE REASONS FOR SUFFERING

Once we have adjusted our focus onto God rather than Job and understood the basic nature of the accusations that are being made concerning God's policies, we can begin to see that righteousness is more under consideration than is suffering. The question asked is, "Why is Job righteous?" not, "Why is Job suffering?" No paradigmatic explanation is offered for why suffering takes place, but there is a lot of interest in what constitutes righteousness. We don't have to understand Job's suffering; we do have to understand his righteousness. His suffering does not give us direction about our suffering, but his reasons for righteousness should make us think about our reasons for righteousness. Will Job's righteousness be sustained even when God's policies are incomprehensible and nothing seems to make sense? Will ours? As the book unfolds, we will see that this is the critical issue to be resolved.

Job's pain and anguish lead to a debate as to why he suffers. The human participants all have their opinions about the reason for his suffering and also about how he can get relief. In this debate, they all (Job, the three friends and Elihu) present themselves as wisdom teachers. They claim wisdom and undermine the wisdom of the others.

As we get into the plot of Job, we will see who wins and who loses this debate. Also, how does God enter into the discussion? Indeed, we will see that again this book is not about Job or any of the human participants, whose wisdom is shown to be woefully inadequate, but about God himself, who alone is wise.

STUDYING THE BOOK OF JOB

As we proceed, how do we go beyond a surface reading of the book? First, we must remember that the book of Job was written not to us in the twenty-first century A.D. but centuries ago to an ancient Israelite audience. That does not mean that the book does not speak to us today; certainly it does. The church recognizes the book of Job as canonical—that is, as a standard of our faith and practice—but we must understand the book on its own terms in order to comprehend its significance for the modern believer. How do we do that?

We must first recognize that the book of Job was written in Hebrew—not modern Hebrew, but ancient Hebrew. Thus, we begin with a translation of Job in our vernacular, which for most of the present readers is English. Translation itself involves interpretation, but for our purposes we are going to depend upon a translation, and of course we will be presenting quotations of the book of Job in English.

But much study remains to be done even using the English text of Job. Since the book is a product of the ancient Near East, we are helped by placing the book in the context of the ancient Near East. We are also helped by studying the book as a piece of literature—by determining its literary type or genre, inspecting its structure and exploring the style of writing.

The book of Job is also a work of theology; that is, it speaks about God and humanity's relationship with God. Our study of Job will emphasize a theological analysis of the book. It is important to read the book on its own, but ultimately we want to put it in the broader context of the Bible as a whole, and for the Christian that will include the New Testament. Thus, we will explore how the book of Job addresses us as Christian readers. This concern will lead us to inquire not only how the book might anticipate Jesus Christ (Lk 24:25-27, 44-49) but also what relevance the book might have for how we think and act today.

In summary, the book of Job can be studied at a variety of significant levels, and we will be interacting with these throughout this book:

- What does the book say (translating the book)?

- How did the author package that message literarily?

- What philosophical/theological points is the book making in its original context?

- How does that message fit together with Christian theology?

- What practical significance does that message have for us today as Christians?

FOR FURTHER REFLECTION

1. What did you think the book of Job was about before you read this chapter?

2. What should we expect to learn from the book of Job?

3. What is on trial in the book of Job?

4. What does it mean when the challenger asks God, "Does Job fear God for nothing?"

5. What is the problem with trying to live in order to benefit from a relationship with God?

6. What is the role of wisdom in the book?

TWO

What Is the
Rhetorical Strategy of
the Book of Job?

Rhetorical strategy refers to the ways in which a book's purpose unfolds section by section. A book has a purpose, a direction, an objective and a focus. Its parts are shaped and arranged in order to achieve that purpose effectively. As readers, we want to track with the book and understand the parts, how they fit together and what each one contributes. This is true of any literature, but it is especially true of the Bible. We believe that the authority of God is vested in the author's purpose and rhetorical strategy, for these are the foundation of the book's message and teaching.

THE PURPOSE OF THE BOOK

We would identify the purpose of the book as *how to think well about God when disaster strikes*. When life is going wrong we would like to know how God governs the world. In the process, we can discover whether our righteousness stands up. The book of Job is going to make the case that God's justice is not the foundation of how the world operates. We cannot explain all circumstances by investigating them as the result of righteous or wicked behavior. The book of Job turns our attention away from the idea that the world runs by God's justice and offers the alternative that, instead of trying to understand everything that happens as a reflection of God's justice, we should learn to trust his wisdom.

It is particularly common for readers to feel disappointed with the speeches of God. They sound to some readers like deflection—a power play in which the real issues are set aside while God simply overwhelms and intimidates Job. In fact it is not uncommon to hear that the answer in the book of Job is, "I am God, and you are not." This generally has an implied complement: "So just shut up," or "Mind your own business," or "I can do what I want," or "You are worthless." A preferable understanding would be, "I am God, who is supremely wise and powerful, so I want you to trust me even when you don't understand."

UNDERSTANDING THE STRUCTURE

To understand the rhetorical strategy of a book, we must understand its structure. This can only be accomplished if we consider the structure to be cohesive and intentional. Though many modern interpreters have found the book lacking in cohesiveness, we would contend that each of the components of the book plays a significant role in the development of the book's purpose. The various styles of literature used by the book include dialogue, discourse, narrative, hymn and lament. All these are woven together into a poignant piece of wisdom literature. None of the parts can be easily written off as later additions or as redundant once we understand the role that each plays in the book. (See figure 2.1.)

Narrative sections (prologue and epilogue) serve as brackets on either end of the book. Just inside those brackets we find Job's lament (Job 3) and Job's closing statements (in Job 40 and 42). The two longest portions of the book are the poetic dialogues and discourses.[1] There are three cycles of dialogue and three sets of discourses (Job, Elihu and God). Among the most difficult decisions about the structure of the book is what to do with Job 28. Opinions vary, but one of the most common views, and the one that we are most persuaded by, is that this wisdom hymn is best regarded as coming from the narrator rather than from any of the characters. As such, it serves as a pivot point in the book. It provides a conclusion to the dialogues and a transition to the discourses.[2] Though the hymn is

Narrative Frame: Job 1–3		
	Prologue: Heaven and earth	1–2
	Job's opening lament	3
	Cycle One: Job 4–14	
	Eliphaz	4–5
	Job	6–7
	Bildad	8
	Job	9–10
	Zophar	11
	Job	12–14
	Cycle Two: Job 15–21	
Dialogue	Eliphaz	15
	Job	16–17
	Bildad	18
	Job	19
	Zophar	20
	Job	21
	Cycle Three: Job 22–27	
	Eliphaz	22
	Job	23–24
	Bildad	25
	Job	26–27
Interlude: Wisdom Hymn, Job 28		
	Series One: Job 29–31	
	Job: Reminiscences	29
	Job: Affliction	30
	Job: Oath of innocence	31
	Series Two: Job 32–37	
Discourses	Elihu: Introduction and theory	32–33
	Elihu: Verdict on Job	34
	Elihu: Offense of Job	35
	Elihu: Summary	36–37
	Series Three: Job 38–41	
	Yahweh: Maintaining roles and functions in cosmic order	38–39
	Yahweh: Illustrations from cosmic order	40:6–41:34
Narrative Frame: Job 42		
	Job's closing statements	(40:3-5) 42:1-6
	Epilogue: Heaven and earth	42:7-17

Figure 2.1. Structure of the book of Job

positioned between two speeches of Job and gives no clear indication that the speaker has changed, it would represent a jarring departure from the stance that Job has adopted in the dialogue section and would align poorly with the attitude in Job's discourses in Job 29–31.[3] Job's last speech in Job 27:7-23 is pessimistic and even fatalistic and, as such, moves in the opposite direction from the trajectory of Job 28. Furthermore, because Job 29–31 shows no hint of the convictions expressed in Job 28, Job 28 cannot be viewed as simply a new insight. Evidence from the Hebrew speech-introduction formulas can be garnered to support this, and the technical discussion can be found elsewhere.[4]

When we consider the wisdom hymn in the mouth of the narrator, its rhetorical role becomes clear. In Job 4–27, we presume that we have been listening to the wisest men in the world. However, Job 28 indicates that we have not yet heard anything resembling wisdom. Job's refusal to adopt the strategies of the friends and his insistence on pursuing vindication rather than restoration of benefits has shown that he *does* serve God for nothing—it was not the benefits that motivated his fearing God. At this point in the book, then, the first challenge to God's policies has been addressed. The policy of blessing righteous people does not undermine their righteousness. The book will now turn attention to the question of whether it is good policy for righteous people to suffer.

Even though Job, having held to the integrity of his righteousness, has offered a stellar defense, he has not demonstrated wisdom. Wisdom has yet to be heard. Job 28 therefore turns the attention of the book away from the righteousness of God. Instead of focusing on the justice of God, as the discourses of Job and Elihu attempt to do, the book of Job will conclude with the wisdom of God as revealed in God's discourses.

THE TRIANGLE OF TENSIONS IN JOB

A final element of the rhetorical strategy can be unpacked using a triangle diagram that highlights the tensions being worked out in the book. (See figure 2.2.[5])

As long as Job, a righteous man, is prospering, the triangle represents equilibrium—everything is stable. Once Job begins suffering, one of the

corners of the triangle has to be given up. We can follow the progress of
the book as we consider which corner the various parties desire to defend
and which they are willing to release.

Job's friends defend the corner of the retribution principle (the
righteous will prosper, and the wicked will suffer; see full discussion in
chap. 3). They are convinced that the retribution principle is true (see

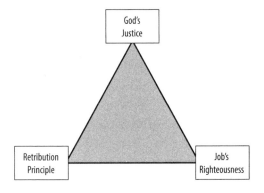

Figure 2.2. Triangle of tensions

figure 2.2). If this is so, then either God is not just or Job is not righteous.
They cannot countenance a world without God's justice, so their doubts
focus on Job's righteousness. They conclude that his lack thereof must be
the weak link and begin probing to discover Job's past sins.

Job, in sharp contrast, defends the corner of his righteousness above
all else. As he considers the merits of the other two corners, he tries to
find weaknesses in the retribution principle. Yet, in the end, he comes to
question the justice of God. This is why he presses for a chance to face
God in court, to hear the accusation read and to defend his righteousness.
Job therefore expresses significant doubts about God's justice.

Elihu takes a stand that differs somewhat from the other friends and
from Job himself. Elihu dramatically defends the corner of God's justice.
Of that he is certain, and in this he is in agreement with the three friends.
But, as with the other characters, he then faces a conundrum about which
of the other corners will be compromised. He cannot find a flaw in the

retribution principle, and he expresses anger over the attempts of the other friends to manufacture some sort of sin in Job's past. Therefore, he devises a creative solution to provide a resolution.

His first move is to redefine the retribution principle. Instead of accepting the normal view that the retribution principle is only a punitive response to past sins (in which case, sins prior to the beginning of the suffering have to be identified), he reconfigures the retribution principle to also include an anticipatory role. On the strength of this reconfiguration, Elihu then turns his attention to Job and proposes that indeed Job may not have committed any great sins in his past. Rather, Job's suffering anticipated and demonstrated an obvious flaw that became evident as his problems unfolded: Job is guilty of self-righteousness.

One could easily conclude that Elihu has gotten it right, but that would be a mistake. God has not had his say as yet. Elihu may be closer than any of the other human characters in the book, and God's position overlaps more with Elihu's position than with any of the others, but Elihu's position still suffers from a major flaw: he continues to believe that justice is the foundation of how the world works. That is a belief that God discards as simplistic. The world's operation is based not on justice but on wisdom. This will be explored more deeply in the following chapters.

FOR FURTHER REFLECTION

1. Why is it important to identify the rhetorical strategy of a book like Job?

2. How would you describe the book's purpose in your own words?

3. How does the structure serve to develop the book's purpose?

4. What is the triangle of tension in the book of Job?

THREE

JOB IN THE CONTEXT OF THE ANCIENT NEAR EAST

J̲ob is not an Israelite. He is from the land of Uz, which is likely located in the land known as Edom in the Bible. However, in many ways Job thinks like an Israelite and believes what Israelites were supposed to believe.[1] The book is distinctly Israelite (and almost certainly written by an Israelite), as it stands in sharp contrast to many of the common beliefs elsewhere in the ancient Near East. The genre of the book is a relatively common one in the ancient Near East (wisdom book featuring a pious sufferer),[2] but the answers that the book eventually offers transcend anything that was proposed in the ancient Near East and would have been truly inconceivable without the revolutionary concept of God that developed in Israel.

SHARED GENRE: WISDOM BOOKS FEATURING A PIOUS SUFFERER

In the Mesopotamian exemplars, the persons suffering are pious in every way known to them, are innocent of wrongdoing as far as they know and are confused about why their god has deserted them. In the cultures of Mesopotamia, offenses were generally assumed to have taken place in the realm of ritual. For example, a Neo-Assyrian prayer expresses an individual's confusion over all that is going wrong in his life.[3] He begins listing all the unintentional ways that he might have offended some deity or other: Did he accidentally step on sacred space of some known or unknown god? Did he perhaps eat some food forbidden by a known or unknown god? Presumably, the sufferer would know if he had committed an ethical offense (e.g., theft, adultery), but pleasing the gods in the ancient world was more concerned with ritual than with ethics. It would be easy to commit ritual offenses without knowing it. If any ritual offense took place, the god might well abandon a person and thereby withdraw his protection, leaving the person vulnerable to all sorts of trouble.

From a literary perspective, the several works dealing with pious suffering from the ancient world do not manifest either the subtlety or complexity found in the book of Job. Nothing suggests any sort of literary dependence between them (though the dialogue of the *Babylonian Theodicy* may have suggested the dialogue form of the book of Job). These other works simply deal with similar scenarios, but the scenario is one that is common in any culture from any period. The most similar pieces of literature date to the second millennium B.C. (see figure 3.1).

When we compare these works to the book of Job, we find similarities that are, for the most part, superficial. An individual is suffering and does not know why. A defense is made before friends or family, and the case is set before God. The sufferer seeks to understand the gods and sometimes engages with a mediator who will help bring resolution. In most cases, they are eventually restored. The differences, however, are extensive and deeply ingrained. They will be explored in the next few sections.

JOB THINKS LIKE AN ISRAELITE: THE GREAT SYMBIOSIS

Job never shows any inclination toward polytheism. In fact, in his oath of innocence he specifically denies having shown homage to the sun or moon (presumably the sun god or moon god; Job 31:24-28). Anyone but Israelites in the ancient world would have readily acknowledged these cosmic deities, but Job refrains from doing so, indicating an Israelite mentality. He seems to recognize which God has brought him trouble and does not appeal to any other god.

Literature	Status	Condition	Resolution	Outcome	Philosophy	Theology
A Man and His God[a] (Sumerian)	Ignorant of offense	Illness; social outcast	Sins confessed	Restored to health	No sinless child born	Results in hymn of praise
Dialogue Between a Man and His God[b] (Akkadian)	Ignorant of offense	Illness	Text broken	Restored to health	None offered	Divine favor assured
Sufferer's Salvation[c] (Akkadian, from Ugarit)	No comment	Illness; death imminent; omens obscure	No indication	Restored to health	God brought his suffering then brought his healing	Results in hymn of praise to Marduk
Ludlul bēl Nēmeqi[d] (Akkadian)	Conscientious piety; ignorant of offense	Social outcast; omens obscure; illness; protective spirits chased away; demon oppression	Dream appearance	Purification bringing appeasement; offenses borne away; demons expelled; restored to health	Gods are inscrutable	Results in hymn of praise to Marduk
Babylonian Theodicy[e] (Akkadian)	Claims piety	Family gone; poverty	None	None	Purposes of gods remote; retribution principle unreliable	Gods make people with evil inclinations and prone to suffering
Job (Hebrew)	Claims righteousness and conscientious piety	Family taken; social outcast; illness; wealth taken	Yahweh offers new perspective based on wisdom	Restoration at all levels but no concluding praise of God	Retribution principle unreliable; divine wisdom is foundation	God's justice is granted given his wisdom

Figure 3.1. Mesopotamian literature compared with Job[f]

[a]*Context of Scripture* (hereafter COS), ed. William W. Hallo and K. Lawson Younger Jr. (Leiden: Brill, 2003), 1:179, ll. 573-75.
[b]*Before the Muses: An Anthology of Akkadian Literature*, 3rd ed. (Bethesda, MD: CDL, 2005), 1:78-80.
[c]*COS*, 1:152, l. 486.
[d]Ibid., 1:153, ll. 486-92.
[e]Ibid., 1:154, ll. 492-95.
[f]The Egyptian literature is not of a similar sort. The "Dialogue Between a Man and His Ba" is more reminiscent of Ecclesiastes, while the Admonitions pieces are about chaos at the society level more than about a single pious person's experiences with suffering. All these pieces would have individual points of comparison but overall do not address the same sort of scenario faced by Job and the Mesopotamian sufferers.

When we turn our attention to the way Job thinks about his suffering, we again find Israelite premises. Sufferers in the ancient Near East stood ready to acknowledge offense as soon as they were shown what it was. They were inclined to believe that they *had* committed an offense. In contrast, Job never considers the possibility that he deserves his suffering. His certainty of his righteousness and his concurrent search for vindication would be commonplace for an Israelite but uncharacteristic for other peoples of the ancient world. Indeed, the whole book revolves around Job thinking like an Israelite.

Job's refusal to acknowledge any offense that might have caused his downfall is yet another pivotal element explored in the book. In most of the ancient world, people believed that they had been created to provide for the gods, who needed food (sacrifices), drink (libations), housing (temples), clothing and all the luxuries connected to their opulent lifestyle. Besides offering a reason for human existence, this understanding also defined human religious responsibility to the gods. And, since the gods needed them, the gods in turn were obliged to provide food and protection for their worshipers. The gods and the people were therefore in a codependent relationship that we can call the *great symbiosis*.

Job, in contrast, shows no great-symbiosis thinking. More than that, the whole premise of the book turns on a denial of the great symbiosis. The foundational question of the book raised in Job 1:9 concerns whether Job serves God for nothing. No one in the ancient Near East served God for nothing. The great symbiosis assumed that people served the gods so that the gods could serve them, and vice versa. In fact, if Job were to betray any evidence of great-symbiosis thinking, the challenge to God's policies would be shown to be accurate. Furthermore, the speeches of the friends show a similarity to the thinking that is found in the ancient Near East, and Job succeeds by resisting their misguided solutions.

THE BOOK OF JOB REFLECTS AN ISRAELITE PERSPECTIVE

The first difference with the ancient Near East that we can observe is in the nature of the individual's suffering. In the examples from the ancient Near East, the suffering is primarily ill health that brings the person to the brink of death. The greater emphasis in Job is the loss of material goods and status in the community. This focus is only a matter of degree, however, since Job's situation would not have been foreign to the rest of the ancient world.

An even more important difference can be found when we consider the nature of the offense. The question of the book concerns Job's righteousness and never raises the possibility that he has been derelict in his ritual duties or that he committed some sort of ceremonial offense. Again, this stands in sharp contrast to the rest of the ancient Near East and shows that the book reflects an Israelite way of looking at the world and at the relationship between God and humans.

In a world where ritual offense is the most common sort of affront to the gods, the usual response is appeasement. The basic assumption is that the god has become angry for having been neglected or through some desecration of sacred space, and appeasement must therefore be made (a ritual response) so that his anger may be assuaged. The gods of the ancient Near East were considered somewhat unpredictable and inexplicably moody. In contrast, Yahweh is not portrayed as angry, nor does anyone (neither Job nor his friends) consider appeasing him with offerings. Unlike his Mesopotamian counterparts, Job never considers the option that he deserves what he is experiencing.

Another way in which the book maintains an Israelite way of thinking in contrast to a generally ancient Near Eastern perspective is that neither God's justice nor the sufferer's righteousness is featured in the ancient Near East, whereas both are the central elements in the book of Job. Lacking clear revelation from their gods, the people of the ancient Near East could not know the gods' standards of righteousness. Such standards could not be identified by contemplating the nature of the gods, for the gods did not exhibit consistent or commendable behavior. In the ancient Near East, piety (by which we refer to conscientiousness in ritual activity) was far more in focus than any presumed standard of righteousness. Orthopraxy (proper performance) was far more important than orthodoxy (right belief). Whether by prayers, laments or rituals, deity is eventually appeased in the Mesopotamian pieces. The epilogue of Job is thus interesting in this regard, as Yahweh *is* angry with the friends (not with Job), and the friends are directed to offer a sacrifice and Job will pray for them in order to appease that anger (Job 42:7-9). Those who have represented the ancient Near Eastern way of thinking are given the answers of the ancient Near East and are treated according to the ancient Near Eastern pattern. There is a difference even in this regard, however, since Yahweh is angry not because they have neglected some ritual but because they have not spoken appropriately (Job 42:8).

Job's righteousness is certainly under consideration as the book is constructed, but so is God's justice. The justice of the gods was not relevant to sufferers in the ancient Near East—the only question was whether the gods would disclose the offense and receive the gifts that would turn them away from their anger. The system worked this way not because the gods were just but because they were needy. The gods in the ancient world did not care about defending their character; they were concerned to preserve their prerogatives and their executive perquisites. When the gods did not receive the cultic rites to which they were entitled, their status was threatened and their wrath or abandonment was predictable.

The early declaration of Job's righteousness provides yet another indication that the book is constructed with an Israelite audience in mind. In the extant Mesopotamian manuscripts, no ancient Near Eastern sufferers are ever declared innocent or righteous; they are merely ignorant of what misdeed they might have committed. The deliberation that the book involves is not possible if Job is not identified as righteous from the beginning. Anything less would give the reader the option of concluding that Job actually was suffering because of something that he did. Only in an Israelite perspective could such an extreme claim be made.

Another topic that distinguishes the Israelite book of Job from its nearest Mesopotamian analogues has to do with the topic of wisdom. We have observed that the book of Job is concerned to point out the inadequacy of human wisdom and the primacy of divine wisdom. The human attempts to diagnose Job's problem and discover its remedy fail miserably. In response, God appears to Job and compels him to live in mystery, not giving an answer to his suffering but asserting his own wisdom and power.

Other ancient Near Eastern texts do not even come close to such a transcendent view of divinity.

ANSWERS OFFERED IN THE ANCIENT NEAR EAST AND IN JOB

In the ancient Near East, the answers that were offered ranged from divine inscrutability to the inherent sinfulness of humanity to gods who made humanity crooked. Job himself considers some of these, but the book of Job does not defend any of them. In the ancient Near East, people believed that no one could accomplish everything that the gods required, so there would always be something to anger the gods. Nothing could be done about this but strive for a higher degree of piety and call out for mercy upon the inevitable failure.

When it came to placing blame in the ancient Near East, then, there was nowhere to turn. People were not to blame if the gods were less than forthcoming about their requirements. Gods could not be blamed for their capriciousness or their fickleness—that was just who they were. Furthermore, if they removed their protection in their anger, they were not the ones who necessarily caused the suffering. The removal of divine protection made a person vulnerable to demonic attack, a demonic role absent from Old Testament theology, including in Job.[4] These demons were not seen as doing the will of the deity; they were simply acting in character by attacking a vulnerable subject. Neither could the demons be blamed for their actions, since they were merely creatures who wreaked havoc by their nature. Consequently, the suffering of the pious was simply a possibility that was inherent in the nature of the gods as understood by those who blindly attempted to serve them. The system is summarized poignantly in the best-known exemplar of the pious sufferer from the ancient Near East, the piece known as Ludlul Bēl Nēmeqi ("I Will Praise the God of Wisdom"):

> I wish I knew that these things were pleasing to one's god!
> What is proper to oneself is an offence to one's god;
> What in one's own heart seems despicable is proper to one's god.
> Who knows the will of the gods in heaven?

Who understands the plans of the underworld gods?
Where have mortals learnt the way of a god?[5]

In the book of Job, one cannot conclude that Job deserves his suffering; thus, innate human sinfulness or inclination to sin, even inadvertently, will not stand. Neither can one deduce that God is inscrutable and therefore acting without any guiding principles. The book neither considers that one's suffering is directly related to one's actions nor claims that God is imprinting his justice on the world of our experience. His role in causation is affirmed but not in terms of micromanaging day-to-day occurrences.

At the same time, the book does not revert to a deistic position in which God is uninvolved. The answers the book offers do not relate to human nature or to divine nature but rather offer an understanding of God's policies. By observing what the typical ancient Near Eastern solutions were, we can gain a greater understanding of the answers this book offers. In fact, the typical answers we find in the ancient Near East are not all that different from those that we find in our modern world. It is therefore important that we come to recognize their inadequacies.

SUMMARY AND CONCLUSION

With so many important differences, it is remarkable that some could still suggest that the book of Job borrows from the ancient Near Eastern exemplars, except that perhaps these exemplars provide the inspiration for the form of a debate or dialogue (as in the *Babylonian Theodicy*), but not the substance of the book. A more defensible model sees the mentality of ancient Near Eastern literature as a foil for the book of Job. Job's friends are the representatives of the ancient Near Eastern perspective, and their views are soundly rejected. Nevertheless, we would have a poorer understanding of the book of Job if we did not look at it against its ancient Near Eastern backdrop. The world of the ancient Near East helps us to understand the way the book is framed and the issues with which it is dealing. As we have become familiar with the literature of the ancient Near East, we have discovered the book of Job's conversation partners. Our understanding of the book of Job is necessarily truncated if we have no awareness of the dialogue to which it contributes.

In conclusion, we can summarize the distinctly Israelite features in Job:

- No great symbiosis (God does not have needs; see Job 22:3)
- Interest in justice of God
- Interest in righteousness as an abstract concept
- A sense of personal righteousness that goes beyond that which the ancient world would have provided
- No ritual offenses considered or ritual remedies suggested or pursued
- No appeasement pursued
- Divine wisdom as a major theme

FOR FURTHER REFLECTION

1. List the ancient Near Eastern compositions that bear some similarity to Job.

2. How are they similar and dissimilar from the book of Job?

3. Describe the great symbiosis. How does the book of Job contrast with other ancient Near Eastern texts in regard to the great symbiosis?

4. How does knowledge of the ancient Near Eastern literary background help us understand the book of Job better?

FOUR

IS JOB A REAL PERSON?

Readers often come away from the book of Job wondering whether the story is a work of fiction or set in history. In other words, is Job a historical or a literary character, and does it make any difference to the message of the book? This question takes us again to the issue of the genre of the book.

THE GENRE OF THE BOOK OF JOB

The genre of a book tells us how to read it, and thus genre is arguably one of the most important discussions for our understanding of a book. Genres have their own conventions and come with their own assumptions. The signals can be as blatant as referring to something as a parable (for example, Mt 13:24) or an apocalypse (Rev 1:1) or as subtle as the nuances found in how the text presents itself. Genre identification allows us to place a literary work among those that share its nature (whether in form, content or rhetorical theme), and thereby we become informed readers who can receive the full force of the author's communicative intentions. Through certain signals, the author communicates to the reader, who is expected to understand his or her writing. A common but helpful example is the phrase "once upon a time," which signals that the following work is a fairy tale.

Because we are removed in time and culture from ancient literature such as Job, we may find ourselves with uncertainties. Such uncertainties are exacerbated by the possibility that there may be genre categories in antiquity that have no exact correspondence with modern categories. Incomplete understanding of the genres of ancient literature increases the possibility that we might incorrectly impose our own genre label on a work, resulting in distortion.

Yet questions concerning the nature and genre of the book are far more complex than simply determining whether Job really existed and underwent such suffering. In approaching this question, we must keep foremost in our minds that this book is manifestly and unarguably in the genre category of wisdom literature rather than historical literature.[1] As wisdom literature, it makes no claims about the nature of the events; rather, it provides a "thought experiment" (see discussion below) in order to explore an important question. Consequently, the discussion about whether the events are real events is misplaced. The author is using the various parts of the book to pose a philosophical scenario that will be used to address wisdom themes such as suffering and the retribution principle.[2] We would be mistaken to think that the author seeks to unfold a series of historical events. This is, after all, wisdom literature.[3] As wisdom literature (and, more specifically, a wisdom debate addressing the question of the source of true wisdom), it seeks to give us appropriate foundations for understanding how the world works and how God works in the world, not how things work in heaven.

But is this a true story? Was Job a real person in a real past? The Bible contains all sorts of literature, and therefore we cannot assume that Job must be a person who actually lived just because the story is in the Bible. After all, the good Samaritan did not actually live, yet the story presents truth. Since the book of Job is unanimously classified as wisdom literature, nothing of the truth of the book is lost if it is not a reflection of historical events. Job's suffering is not redemptive, but rather didactic; it provides an occasion for an important discussion about motivations for righteousness, wisdom and suffering.

At the same time, wisdom literature can employ real life people and their circumstances. From the beginning, then, we can conclude that the truth of the book does not depend on the historical nature of its story, which means historicity does not matter. Yet we can explore the issue as a curiosity.

First, one can observe that at least some parts of the book are the result of literary art. This is particularly true of the speeches. The highly poetic nature of the speeches indicates that they do not depict people speaking extemporaneously; these are carefully constructed pieces of literary expression. Even if people could speak this way, one would not expect to find a stenographer on the scene to record these dialogues. We can safely conclude that they do not represent real, spontaneous conversations.

At the same time, we might ask whether the book still expects its readers to believe that a man named Job actually existed—a man who was unbelievably wealthy, successful in every way, godly above any other person alive, who suffered loss of all but his life and who then had it all restored. In wisdom literature that has evidence of literary construction at some points, we cannot simply assume as a default position that this is a real story of a real person. Nevertheless, some evidence exists that the author would like us to think so. Real places are mentioned (Uz, Buz, Teman) as are real people groups (Sabeans, Chaldeans). But these are remote, faraway places to the audience, and therefore could be used literarily. Remember that in the parable of the good Samaritan, real types of people and real places are used for the setting.

JOB ELSEWHERE IN THE BIBLE

Once we move outside the book, we find reference made to Job in two other biblical books: Ezekiel and James. In Ezekiel, he is identified as a paragon of righteousness along with Noah and Daniel (Ezek 14:14, 20).[4] In James, Job is noted for his patience or, as some versions translate it, his perseverance (Jas 5:11). For some, these references are enough to indicate that Job was a real person in a real past, though others are willing to accept these as references to a literary character. Consequently, we could say that these references offer evidence that Job truly existed even if they fall short of proving it absolutely. These later references could simply be looking back on the story as an example that would still be effective even if Job were not historical. For instance, we could and do appeal to the example of the good Samaritan as an example of compassion even though the good Samaritan was not a historical figure. So, at best, these references to Job in other biblical books affirm only the very basic details: he was righteous, and he persevered through suffering. That would still leave room for most of the book of Job to be constructed literarily around this well-known ancient worthy.

THE CONSTRUCTION OF LEGENDS FROM HISTORICAL FIGURES

We know that there are legendary figures in the ancient world, but there is no reason to believe that the legends are not built around historical persons (e.g., Gilgamesh, Adapa, Etana, Kirtu).[5] Though there may be purely literary characters in the literature of the ancient world, ancient authors were more likely to construct their literature around epic figures of the distant past than to fabricate fiction as we understand it today.[6] This practice is illustrated in the Mesopotamian wisdom work known as Ludlul Bēl Nēmeqi ("I Will Praise the God of Wisdom"), a first-person narration of one who has suffered greatly and does not know why. His name can be deduced from the work, and analysts do not hesitate to consider him a real person.[7] Weiss builds the case that the introduction of Job's name indicates syntactically that Job's character and reputation are familiar to all.[8] All of this would support the notion that Job was an historical figure—a man who was righteous and suffered greatly.[9] We lose nothing by accepting Job's story as historical, and we gain nothing by concluding that he is a fabricated, fictional character. But these statements could be switched and remain true.

A THOUGHT EXPERIMENT

For the sake of conversation, then, let us assume that a righteous, prosperous, suffering and restored Job really existed but that the speeches in the book are literary constructs. We would then be compelled to ask about the character of the rest of the book. Which parts are reports of historical events, and which parts are literary constructs? Since there is clearly some literary construction in the book, any part of the book could conceivably be so classified. As there is no external or internal verification that other parts are to be considered factual, we have only our own judgment to go on. Remember, the teachings of the book are true regardless.

One suggestion has been that the book constitutes a thought experiment in which a philosophical idea can be discussed based on a hypothetical scenario.[10] One could conceivably build a thought experiment around the general circumstances of a real person's experiences. But the factors that set up the scenario must be carefully constructed for a thought experiment to work well. In the case of Job, we find such careful construction in the extremes that frame the conversation. It would not be sufficient for Job to be simply a generally righteous man; he must be the most righteous man that lived—otherwise, the audience might imagine that there is indeed some offense that brought on his suffering. It would not be sufficient for Job to be a fairly successful man who then had a downturn in his circumstances. For the issues to be addressed, he must be prosperous beyond imagination so that his ruin is the worst imaginable. It would not be sufficient for Job to have gradually suffered losses of wealth, family and health. The losses tumbling in on top of one another make clear that these are not just the ordinary misfortunes of life. All these extremes sharpen our focus as readers and eliminate any easy answers as we consider the important philosophical and theological issues the book wants to engage. The extreme nature of all these details suggests that they are the result of a literary construction designed to bring the issues into sharp relief.

But what about the role of God? The scene in heaven likewise supplies some essential extremes. God's strong affirmation of Job's righteousness demonstrates that the reader can allow no reservations here. Job *is* righteous, and God is not lashing out at him because of some hidden fault. This eliminates some of the easy answers found in ancient Near Eastern literature (and ones that we can easily concoct for ourselves or for people we know who are suffering). Furthermore, we cannot account for Job's suffering by imagining spiritual forces working independently, again eliminating any easy explanations. God takes full responsibility (Job 2:3), and neither Job nor his friends ever consider the possibility that God was simply uninvolved.

We therefore adopt the position that, though Job himself may have been a real person who actually lived, the rest of the book is a literary work of art providing a wisdom discussion that is framed by extremes. In this view, even the scene in heaven is part of the literary construct and as such offers an extreme view of God. If that is so, we cannot deduce anything about God from the behavior portrayed in that scene. This is important for some readers because it is easy to get distracted by this picture of a God who is "making wagers with the devil" or who has no knowledge of what Satan is doing or of what motivates Job's righteousness. Instead, we should take this scenario as a hypothetical one: What if we imagine . . . ? In this view, the truth of the message of Job is preserved while potential concerns about the nature of God are avoided. This allows us to consider the extreme and artificial scenario the author has constructed so that we can engage in a deep investigation of an important philosophical issue without having to continually cope with the muddied waters of the normal ambiguities of people and their circumstances. Whether we label it a thought experiment or simply a hypothetical scenario built around extremes, we can encounter the God-given message of the text undistracted from incidental curiosities and without the angst that comes with wondering why God killed Job's children.

WHO WROTE JOB AND WHEN?

In the ancient world, even a masterpiece such as this typically remains anonymous. The ancient world did not afford authorship the same significance given it in the modern world and so paid little attention to it. Authority figures (kings, prophets, etc.) were attributed, but they were rarely the ones who actually penned the literature. We do not know who the author of this masterpiece is or when it was written. A few details suggest that the setting is in an ancient time. The idea that Job lived in the time of the Patriarchs is often suggested because of the absence of any reference to covenant or Torah and because Job, as patriarch of his clan, serves as priest for his family with no mention of a temple. But all of that would be true of someone outside of Israel in any period, and Job, as we have noted, is presented as a non-Israelite.

Even if we could locate the events in a time period with confidence, that would say nothing about the date of the composition of the book. As we have indicated above, the book clearly shows Job thinking like an Israelite and features Israelite perspectives. It is undoubtedly addressed to an Israelite audience. All these factors would suggest a date of composition long after any date when Job himself would have lived. Judgments about the dating of the composition therefore can only rely on subtle internal observations or an assessment of the language of Job.

With regard to the language, we likewise have little basis for a confident conclusion. The book is uncontested for the complexity of its Hebrew. Scholars have attempted to identify it as a dialect or even as a translation, but no such suggestions have been substantiated or widely accepted.[11] All of this to say that until we have more to go on, we cannot use the language of the book to determine its date. In the end, the book does not offer sufficient evidence to identify a date for either the presumed life of Job or for the composition of the book; its truths are timeless, and it functions as Scripture regardless of the date of the setting or of the composition.

FOR FURTHER REFLECTION

1. Why is it important to determine the genre of the book of Job?

2. How would you describe its genre? And what effect does this identification have on your interpretation of the book?

3. After reading this chapter, do you think Job was a real person? And does it matter to the message of the book? Why or why not?

4. How does thinking of the book as a thought experiment affect the way we interpret the book?

GETTING TO KNOW THE CHARACTERS OF THE BOOK OF JOB

■　　■　　■

FIVE

WHAT DO WE
LEARN ABOUT GOD FROM
THE BOOK OF JOB?

God has often taken a beating at the hands of readers of the book of Job. He is portrayed as unaware of Satan's intent; he wagers with a man's life; he ruins Job without cause (by his own admission), including wiping out his family; and he ignores Job's repeated pleas for some explanation of the charges that brought his undoing. In the end he intimidates Job with what is perceived to be an I-am-God-and-you're-not speech, tells Job how he made two creatures of legendary power and mystery, and then restores Job's prosperity with no defense or explanation. Who would tolerate such a God, let alone revere him? Response to a God like this gives real meaning to the concept of "fearing God." Is this the portrait of God in the book of Job? If so, we might well wonder how the book came to be canonized in the first place.

This is an important issue because we believe that the primary significance of the Bible as Scripture is that it offers a normative revelation of God. Our task as readers is to submit to the authority of God's Word above all by adopting the picture of God that it delivers to us. Consequently, if the book of Job is offering a revelation of God that includes the elements in the previous paragraph, we have some real challenges.

We can therefore suggest that the most important question is this:

What does the book of Job reveal about God? The teaching about God must first be derived from a careful literary reading of the book. That means that its genre and rhetorical strategy take center stage. We cannot learn from a book theologically until we understand it literarily. With that in mind we need to distinguish between the literary scenario of the book and the message of the book. The literary scenario portrays what could be considered a necessary caricature of God while the message conveys inspired teaching about God's operation of the world: how it does and does not work, and what our posture toward God ought to be.

LITERARY CARICATURE

Does Yahweh really make Job a bona fide offer to be God-for-a-day in Job 40:10-14? Most readers can easily identify that offer as a rhetorical device rather than God's true willingness to put the universe into someone else's hands. The scene in heaven in Job 1–2 is no less literary and rhetorical than the one on earth in Job 38–41. That means that the message of the book and the revelation about God cannot be derived from those literary constructions. The scenario is built on extremes—unnatural situations—so that the message of the book can be developed.

1. Does God need to be informed about Satan's activities? No. The author uses conventional thinking about how the heavenly council operates in order to stage the conversation that sets the scene. Yahweh is portrayed as a royal figure who receives reports from the functionaries to whom tasks have been delegated. In other words, the description of heaven is modeled after an ancient Near Eastern royal court. The angels are his court officials—his divine council—and the challenger ("Satan," see chap. 6) is a spy, a member of the heavenly CIA. This is a literary motif, and we do not need to believe that God actually works this way. Even if he did, there would be no reason to believe that his question reveals his ignorance. His question is intended merely to receive a report and evoke a response.

2. Does God involve himself in a wager with the devil? No, on numerous counts. We will discuss the identity of the challenger in the next

chapter. Regarding the wager, the author is not offering us revelation about how God operates. The literary role played by the wager is to demonstrate from the start that Job's suffering is not the result of anything he has done.

3. Does God have to find out what Job's motivations really are? No. The question being resolved for the readers is not, Will the most righteous man ever known maintain his righteousness when his world falls apart? The text is offering answers to *our* questions, not to God's uncertainties. Readers have no benefit in being told that God knows that Job's motivations are pure because it is not Job who is our ultimate concern. As readers, we are investigating how God's justice interacts with our experiences and circumstances. The book is concerned with what *we* need to discover, not with what God needs to discover.

4. Does God care about Job? That is, should we infer God's relative care for Job from his question, "Have you considered my servant Job?" We cannot deduce God's "feelings" about Job from his introduction of the conversation about Job. Everything in the scene in heaven is artificial—a scenario designed to set the scene literarily. The characters need to be considered as characters in a story.[1]

5. Is God uncaring about Job as he launches his ruin? No. The literary scenario holds all such assessments at bay.

6. Does God violently wipe out Job's children? There is no reason to consider God as careless with human lives simply to make a point. It is essential that the extremes of Job's suffering be portrayed as convincingly as the extremes of his righteousness and his prosperity. Nothing less than total loss would provide the necessary factors for the wisdom instruction that is the focus. Again, it is instructive to use the same sort of thinking that we use when we encounter Jesus' parables, which examine realistic issues by constructing situations that mix realism with extreme, exaggerated or unbelievable factors.[2] These extremes provide one of the telltale signs that we are dealing with a literary construction.

7. Does God heartlessly ignore Job's pleas? It is clear that God is unresponsive, but the book and its teaching would flounder badly if Job succeeded in drawing God into litigation. That God is impervious to such pleas does not make him heartless; it shows that this is not the path to a solution. The message that the book intends to convey is not achieved by God giving explanations; in fact, that would destroy the message of the book. The posture of God therefore has nothing to do with whether he is emotionally responsive to Job.

8. Does God intimidate Job into silence? In Yahweh's speeches he is undeniably portrayed as intimidating—given that he is God, *intimidating* does not begin to capture his nature. But, does the author intend for the reader to be cowed into abject groveling as the appropriate response to this Wizard of Oz power play? If the book of Job is suggesting a portrait of God that conveys, "How dare you approach me?" it would stand in sharp contrast to the book of Psalms in which, by the example of the psalmists, God is approachable with all sorts of concerns. We would therefore again maintain that this posture of Yahweh is necessary as a literary means rather than as a theological end. The point is not that God is unapproachable but that he is irreducible. Yahweh wraps himself in a storm not because Job dares to question him but because Job has been willing to make his own righteousness and his own perceptions of the operations of the cosmos the basis by which God's actions can be assessed. It is on this specific point that the message of the book comes into play.

Parables show a similar resistance to being interpreted as providing portraits of God. When we consider numerous parables in which God is represented by the characters in the parable, we would be remiss to think that any of them are intended to tell us what God is really like. For example,

• From the parable of the workers in the vineyard (Mt 20), we could not infer that God (portrayed as the landowner) actually works this way. The payment of wages does not have direct correlation to how people are treated in heaven. The same wage offered to those who worked only the last hour is an intentional exaggeration to highlight the point the parable is making.

- In the parable of the shrewd manager (Lk 16), the master's response to his manager's currying favor should not suggest how God wants us to act. God's character is not being revealed as a shrewd operator.

- In the parable of the unmerciful servant (Mt 18:21-35), the parable actually ends with, "This is how my heavenly Father will treat each of you." Yet we cannot help but notice that the master hands the servant over for torture until he can repay (Mt 18:34). Here readers perceive a subtle difference between the message of the parable and the nature of God.

- Perhaps the clearest example of this principle is found in the parable of the late-night request (Lk 11:5-8). Here the character that represents God is reluctant to help and needs to be badgered into action by the nagging of the one in need. Surely this would be an extreme portrayal of God in order to make a point.

We conclude that we would not use any of these story elements to provide sound theological teaching about the nature of God. *God is a character in the book of Job, and it is important to examine what the author does with the character rather than what the character does.* To extract that teaching, we look to the message of the book.

THE MESSAGE ABOUT GOD IN THE BOOK OF JOB

The authoritative information about God revealed in the book of Job comes through the message that the book offers rather than through the rhetorical shape of the literary character. In the message of the book, points are being made about God's justice, God's wisdom and God's policies.

God's justice is portrayed as an accepted fact, but it is also indiscernible. Technically, one should not claim that God is just—that appears to make him accountable to an external system. It is also a less-than-meaningful statement if we can never really have sufficient information to demonstrate that God is acting justly. Instead, we should say that justice emanates from the person of God. At the same time, however, we recognize that the justice that emanates from him does not stamp itself indelibly on the world in which we live. Consequently, though we affirm that justice is found in him, we cannot base our expectations in life or our understanding of how the world runs on that premise. The book therefore does not contest God's justice but removes it from the table for discussion and focuses attention elsewhere. God does not endow the world with justice, though he is able to enact justice as his wisdom dictates.

God's wisdom is the key to the book's message. As readers are impressed with the wisdom of God, they are encouraged to trust him rather than to try to figure out *why* he is doing what he does. Rather than seeking explanations that will verify his justice, the response to God should be to trust the way he has chosen to have the world operate, trust him regarding the circumstances that come into our lives and trust that his ways are the best ways. That trust may well be based on the firm belief that he loves us, but the book itself does not build the case on that foundation.

God's policies serve as the main focus of the book. Satan's challenge pertains directly to the impact that God's policy of blessing righteous people has on Job's motives for being righteous ("Does Job fear God for nothing?" [Job 1:9]). Job's demands pertain directly to God's policy of allowing righteous people to suffer. Given this literary and theological focus, we must concentrate on what has been revealed about God's policies (and therefore indirectly about God) through the book of Job.

The book promotes the conclusion that the way God operates the world is more complicated than people can imagine and that, therefore, God's way cannot be reduced to a simple equation (such as the retribution principle). Rain falls not only on the just and unjust alike, but it also falls where no one lives (Job 38:25-26). Obviously, then, justice is not the reigning principle, and the retribution principle (see chap. 2) cannot offer a theodicy. The purpose of a theodicy is to give some explanation for the existence of evil and suffering and, in the end, to vindicate God in relation to what people experience in the world. From a theological standpoint positing a theodicy is a questionable undertaking for exactly the same reason that Job is chided. God is not in need of our vindication, nor are we capable of devising a sufficiently comprehensive understanding to which we could hold him accountable. God is not accountable to us.

If a specific principle of justice were the foundation of God's operations, then we might conclude that a theodicy is possible. But that is not the case. Yet at the same time the theological premise underlying the retribution principle is repeatedly affirmed in various books of Scripture. In this regard the book of Job suggests to us that the retribution principle retains some validity as good theology even though it cannot be sustained for theodicy. As theology, the retribution principle remains an affirmation that, as the God of justice, God delights in bringing prosperity and success to those who are faithful to him (though he does not guarantee it). He also takes the sin of the wicked seriously and undertakes their judgment when he deems it appropriate. The retribution principle is therefore not an explanation of how God operates the world, but it is an affirmation about who God is, recognizing that his identity and character are bound to have ramifications in the world. His working out of those ramifications, however, is totally governed by his wisdom. In his wisdom he has created the world as he deemed appropriate, and we trust that wisdom.

We therefore should be able to affirm that God's ways are the best ways. The book offers that conclusion as it ends with Job again being the recipient of God's abundant blessing. This is not the climax to the book—it simply reflects the idea that God's policies are going to continue unmodified, the challenges notwithstanding.

FOR FURTHER REFLECTION

1. Is the idea of the author of Job creating a literary caricature of God troubling to you? Why or why not?

2. How can we distinguish between a literary caricature of God within the book of Job and the book's message about who God is?

3. In the final analysis, what do we learn about God in Job?

SIX

WHO IS "SATAN" IN JOB?

Most English translations refer to the being who is introduced in Job 1:6 as "Satan"—represented as a personal name.[1] Consequently most readers draw the conclusion that this character is the devil, well known to readers of the New Testament. That decision is premature, as will be discussed in this chapter. For the sake of delaying a decision, we will refer to him for now as "the challenger." The challenger is only present in the first two chapters of Job and could therefore be considered a minor character were it not for the fact that he is the catalyst for the scenario that unfolds. He does not stand as an antagonist throughout the book, nor does he have a curtain call at the end. He plays his launching role and then disappears as the story plays out in his wake.

We must not prematurely draw a conclusion on the identity of this character by quickly jumping to the profile of the being we name as Satan in the New Testament. We begin by asking what an Old Testament author or audience would have thought. After all, it is an Old Testament author who has adopted this character and given him a role. What do they know of Satan? Is this "the devil"? Is it a demon? Is it one of the "sons of God" (KJV; NIV translates this phrase as "angels" in Job 1:6)?

Though the Israelites undoubtedly believed in the reality of a demon world, demonology is little attested in the Old Testament. In fact, there is no agreed-upon term for demons.[2] Data gathered from the ancient Near East and throughout the Old Testament would place demons in the terrestrial realm, generally in waste places, having little contact with the legitimate divine realm aside from occasionally being used as instruments for punishment. They tend to have no will or agenda; they only follow their instincts to create havoc. They are amoral. Nothing here matches the information offered about the character identified by the term *satan* in the Old Testament.

EXAMINING THE LEXICAL PROFILE

In the Old Testament the Hebrew word *satan* finds usage both as a verb and as a noun. As a verb it means "to oppose as an adversary," "to challenge" or "to accuse" (Ps 38:20; 71:13; 109:4, 20, 29; Zech 3:1). As a noun it can be applied to a human being, thus designating him an adversary (1 Sam 29:4, "he will turn against us"; 2 Sam 19:22, "interfere"; 1 Kings 5:4; 11:14, 23, 25; Ps 109:6). Finally, in the category of most interest to this study, the noun is applied to celestial beings (Job 1–2 [14x]; Num 22:22, 32; 1 Chron 21:1; Zech 3:1-2 [3x]).

There are no cognates to the Hebrew term in Semitic languages, so they offer no help in unraveling the history of the term. If the technical usage (noun applied to a supernatural being) were original and the other usages developed from it, we would have to conclude, judging from the nuances of those derived terms, that there was little of a sinister nature in the being, for these other usages evidence none of that element. However, the broadly generic sense of the common noun and verb usage suggests that the technical usage is a secondary development.

If this is indeed the case, it would be logical to assume that a supernatural being would have been given this designation as a description of his function, that is, serving as a heavenly adversary. This finds confirmation in the fact that the definite article is attached to the noun in most cases where the noun is applied to a supernatural being. In English, when we refer to someone by means of a proper name, we do not use a definite article (e.g., Sarah, not *the* Sarah). In this practice Hebrew behaves identically. Therefore we must conclude that the individual in Job 1–2 and Zechariah 3:1-2 should be identified as "the challenger" (description of function) rather than as "Satan" (proper name).[3] Beyond the question of translation, however, we must also determine whether this character is the devil—the one who goes by the name of Satan in the New Testament.

We have often extrapolated from the New Testament an understanding that in the Old Testament the technical term *satan* always applies to the *same* supernatural being, a single *satan*. This is easily refuted by the fact that Numbers 22:22 and 32 use the Hebrew word *satan* to refer to the angel of the LORD. Not only can we identify *satan* here as a functional designation, but we can also now consider the possibility that as a function it is not intrinsically evil.[4] Furthermore, since we would not assume that the angel of the LORD is the challenger in every context where the term *satan* occurs, we thereby accept that the challenger is not necessarily always the same supernatural being.

Job 1:6 would lead us to understand that a certain celestial being whose precise identity is unimportant and who has the current and perhaps temporary status of challenger is being introduced into the narrative. Consequently it is possible that the individual designated "the accuser" in Job is not the same individual designated "the accuser" in Zechariah or Chronicles. Though they may be the same being, we cannot simply assume that they must be or that the Israelites would have considered them to be the same individual. Pseudepigraphic literature refers to many *satans*.[5]

THE PROFILE OF THE *SATAN* IN JOB

If we had no name for this individual and had to build his profile from the text of Job, what conclusions could we draw? First, we would observe that the *satan* comes among the sons of God (NIV "angels"). It is clear therefore that he has access to the heavenly throne, and likely he is counted among the members of this heavenly council (Ps 89:5-8),[6] though some have identified him as an intruder. Second, the *satan* does not initiate the discussion of Job; he merely offers an alternative explanation of Job's righteous behavior. Though it is common for the *satan*'s job to be portrayed as seeking out human failings, it is God's policies that are the true focus of the challenge.[7] Job's character is only the test case. In that vein the existence of disinterested righteousness and the effect of a reward system on a person's motives are both very legitimate issues. God does not scoff at the challenge or discount the legitimacy of the question even though the *satan* is challenging God's blueprint for divine-human relations. In other words, the *satan* is questioning the validity of a moral order in which the pious unfailingly prosper. The test of true righteousness would be worship without the promise of reward.[8]

Another question that is affected by whether the *satan* targets God or Job concerns his demeanor toward Job. Some have inferred that the *satan* relished the opportunity to strike at Job. The text does not attribute to God or the *satan* any personal emotional response to Job's tragedy. God has struck Job as much as the *satan* has,[9] and both characters lack any sympathetic response. It would be arbitrary, then, to assume that the *satan* enjoyed Job's suffering while God sadly endured it. There is no expression of glee; there is no diabolical chuckle.

Weiss concludes that nothing intrinsically evil emerges in the author's portrayal of the *satan* in Job. Certainly what he does has negative consequences for Job, a righteous man, but the text makes it clear that God is at least equally responsible for what happens to Job, thus freeing the actions from being implicitly evil.[10] There is no tempting, corrupting, depraving or possessing.

As a result of this profile, we must conclude that we cannot identify the *satan* in Job with the devil, Satan, as we know him in the New Testament, on the premise that they behave similarly. In fact there is little if any overlap between their two profiles. This does not prove that they are *not* the same individual; it merely reduces (if not eliminates) the basis for claiming that they *must* be equated. The profile of the Hebrew *satan* in the book of Job does not answer to the same description as the Satan of the New Testament. While the pictures are not contradictory, and they may even be complementary, we could not consider them homogeneous.

SOCIO-RELIGIOUS PROFILE

The profile of the *satan* in Zechariah 3:1 shows a great deal of similarity to that in Job, so it is important to take a brief look there to see what it contributes to formulating a larger profile. When Joshua the high priest stands before the presence of God, he is confronted by the *satan* and opposed because he is covered with the stains of his and his people's guilt. Is the *satan* wrong to oppose him on this count? Weiss says no:

> True, he "opposes," though not in a spirit of malice, but rather because he meticulously clings to justice, on the principle "Let justice be done though the heavens fall." After all, Joshua the high priest was in fact guilty: he was dressed in garments covered with excrement, and he himself donned them in his guilt. Satan did not garb him in foul clothes through an unjust accusation. The garments are removed when God forgives his sin: he is acquitted not through justice, but through mercy, through pardon.[11]

On the other hand, one significant difference between the scenarios in Job and Zechariah is that the *satan* is rebuked in the latter while in the former he is not.[12] Carol and Eric Meyers contend that this rebuke is not directed against the *satan* performing his function but concerns the evidence he brings.[13] Here again we find the *satan* raising issues concerning God's policies. In Job it is the policy of rewarding the righteous that is being questioned. In Zechariah it is the policy of forgiveness and restoration.[14] Rather than a lengthy test to confirm the legitimacy of God's policy as we have in Job, the *satan* in Zechariah is rebuked on the grounds that punishment had been appropriately accomplished (Joshua is a smoldering brand drawn from the fire; Zech 3:2).

A different profile emerges in other passages. In Numbers 22, 1 Kings 11 and 1 Chronicles 21, the *satan* is viewed as a quasi-independent agent by means of whom punishment is initiated. How does this compare to the profile in Job and Zechariah? In Job and Zechariah, his function is one directed *toward God* in the sense that he initiates challenges concerning God's policies. In these other passages his function is directed *toward humans*. Does the Old Testament deal with two separate profiles or simply two aspects of a single profile? The answer to this question could only be speculative. Again, however, we must note how different the profile(s) is from that which is later provided by the New Testament, where Satan is linked directly to a principle of evil.[15] The New Testament profile reflects the development of thought that took place throughout the intertesta-mental period, traceable through literature that evidences some of the progression in theological thinking that is later affirmed by the New Tes-tament. By the time of the New Testament, much of this thinking had been accumulated into the profile of the one called Satan, the diabolical enemy leading the forces of evil.

The role of the *satan* in Job should be seen as one who acts as a court functionary assigned to investigate the execution of the policies of God—specifically, his policy of blessing the righteous. It is unclear whether he should be seen as a legal opponent, litigant or informant. His challenge strikes right to the heart of the retribution principle, a tenet for which the book seeks to provide a corrective. The *satan's* case is pressed unwittingly by the three friends, for if Job listens to them and confesses to sin simply to appease deity and be restored to favor, the *satan* wins his case. When the role of the friends ends in Job 27, the *satan's* case also is shown to be groundless, and there is no need to mention him again.

The *satan*, this challenger in Job, however, is not an independent agent opportunistically fulfilling his nature. Whatever he does he does through the power of God; all the events of the book are understood as God's ac-tions. He is a character used by the author in ways that correspond to what was known by an Israelite audience. Regardless of whether this is truly the being that the New Testament designates as Satan or the devil, the book of Job needs to be interpreted based on the profile that was available to the target audience. This makes the challenger less theologically sig-nificant in the book. He is not offered as one who can be blamed for Job's suffering, nor does his role provide an explanation for suffering or evil in our experiences or in the world. He is a minor character playing a bit part in the unfolding drama.

The challenger comes among the sons of God, who are the members of the heavenly council (not mere angels, who are messengers for the council). This standing gives him a legitimate status and identifies him as one whom God has delegated to perform certain tasks. The challenge that he brings concerns a potential unintended consequence in the way God acts in the world. He is right about the potential that anticipated reward has for undermining human righteousness. God does not rebuke him; instead, he actively addresses the challenge by giving the challenger freedom to test the system. In that way, Job unknowingly becomes the star witness for the defense of that system. So we now turn our attention to Job.

FOR FURTHER REFLECTION

1. Why is "the challenger" a good translation of *satan*?

2. What exactly does the challenger challenge?

3. Survey as many English translations as you have. How do they translate *satan*? In the light of the argument of this chapter, how do you think it should be rendered?

SEVEN

WHAT IS THE ROLE OF JOB
IN THE BOOK OF JOB?

The book of Job, despite its title, is not about Job. Regardless of all the accolades that we could muster, and there are many, Job's role is in posing the problem of the book rather than in providing answers. Though his comments are less flawed than those of his friends, they are nevertheless flawed. As a character in the book, he represents yet one more wrong way to respond to suffering, and he also illustrates inadequate wisdom. He is commended not for how he responds to suffering but for the quality and motivation of his righteousness. His ideas as to why he suffers (God is unjust) and his prescription for the remedy to his pain (confront God) are both incorrect, thus showing he is not as wise as he thinks.

JOB, THE RIGHTEOUS

In Israel, one of the distinctives of Yahweh is found in the ways that he revealed himself and in the extent of that revelation. One must ask whether the book of Job assumes that revelation. Of course, as a non-Israelite, Job has no knowledge of the Torah or of the covenant with Israel. Yet at the same time it would seem that he has the same sense of obligation to righteousness that is generally sustained as the result of some level of revelation. We will recall for the sake of comparison that, even before the revelation on Mount Sinai, Abram "believed the LORD, and he credited it to him as righteousness" (Gen 15:6). Yet even there it was his belief in the promise of God that was credited to him; Job has no such promises, and his righteousness is not credited to him—it is evident in his behavior. Abram's behavior is emphasized later in Genesis when it is stated that he kept God's commands, decrees and instructions (Gen 26:5)—seeming to imply that he had some special revelation of such things.

Noah is also described as a righteous man (Gen 6:9) even though he had no formal special revelation of God (that we know of) to inform such righteousness. He is more comparable to Job in that his relationship with God is not operating within a covenant. The righteousness of Noah and Job is not a perfect righteousness that is accomplished for Christians by Christ. It is a righteousness that distinguishes them from the world around them. In that sense it is more the sort of righteousness operating in the context of general revelation rather than that which is a response to special revelation. Job 31 serves to give us a workable profile for determining what Job's sense of righteousness entails as he lists all the transgressions of which he claims he is not guilty. Most of what Job claims to his merit are behaviors that would be found commendable (though extreme) in the ancient Near East.

Job's righteousness is what he defends most ardently. His posture on the matter stands in most immediate juxtaposition to the alternative approach of seeking restitution of what he has lost. At issue here is not a precise definition of righteousness but the contrast to benefits. Recall that the challenger has questioned whether Job fears God for nothing. The issue on the table then is whether Job is ultimately interested in what he stands to gain by his righteous behavior or, alternatively, whether he isolates his righteous behavior as having independent value regardless of the benefits. If his righteousness is not motivated by potential gain, what motivates it? The text does not really say because it is primarily interested in establishing whether benefit is the motivator.

We might suggest that a righteousness not motivated by gain would be one that could be motivated either by the expectations of society or by theological factors pertaining to the nature of God. In the former case, an ordered society is a value that is worth pursuing by conforming behavior to its expectations and by actively seeking its stability. In this case, righteousness means being a "team player" in order to achieve an abstract goal. Since the gods also valued stability in society, this motive could also have a theological connection. But it is also possible that a theological motive could be more abstract. If one has an elevated view of God such as that which is articulated in the Old Testament, one's righteousness could potentially be motivated by the belief that righteousness is the appropriate life response to such a God, regardless of the expectations of society or the anticipation of gain.

It is this latter sort of righteousness that characterizes Job, and it is this righteousness that he defends. It leads him to seek vindication. That is, he wants his righteousness to be recognized by everyone but particularly by God. Society would assume that if someone is suffering, especially someone whose fall has been so sudden and complete, he has done something to deserve his fate. Job's recent experiences are therefore considered convincing evidence that he is guilty of serious wrongdoing. He tries to summon God into court so that God can confirm that Job has done nothing to deserve this treatment. This is information that the reader already has. Job is not claiming that he is perfect; he only wants to be declared innocent of the sort of offenses that would have caused his dramatic downfall. He wants to face his judge, hear the charges and be given an explanation or—in the absence of such an explanation—be acquitted.

JOB, THE PIOUS

In the ancient world around Israel, ritual performance was more central to religious duty than was righteousness. In the great symbiosis (see chap. 3) that pervaded the ancient Near East, the gods had needs and people had been created to fill those needs, which they did through ritual acts. The gods were housed, clothed and fed. When people fulfilled these obligations to the gods, the gods in turn made sure that the people were provided for and protected. We will use the word *piety* to refer to this ritual performance.

In this sort of system, people were doing a lot of guessing. They knew that the gods wanted their needs to be met, their sacred space to be respected and their persons to be attended to meticulously. Unfortunately the gods were not forthcoming about exactly what this should look like. One could inadvertently neglect the gods or violate their sacred space and find oneself abandoned and vulnerable. Piety was insurance against the fragile egos of the gods and their volatility. Piety was not mutually exclusive to righteousness but was the one essential for remaining in good standing with the gods. The gods really just wanted to be pampered. They could be easily offended—much to the detriment of the offender—and then would have to be appeased.

Throughout the book of Job this sort of ritual response we are calling piety is never proposed as the needed response to remedy Job's situation. Neither Job nor his friends entertain the possibility that everything could be resolved if Job would only pursue a path of ritual appeasement. Nor is it ever suggested that Job has been guilty of ritual neglect or the violation of sacred space. Piety is not presented as part of the problem nor part of the solution, and it is strangely absent from the conversation. Given these observations we cannot help but notice that the profile of Job in the beginning of the book features an unusual vignette regarding Job's meticulous ritual actions on behalf of his children. We therefore need to take a closer look at Job 1:4-5:

> His sons went and prepared a banquet on their birthday, and they sent invitations to their three sisters to eat and drink with them. After days of feasting had passed, Job would send and consecrate them. Rising early in the morning, he offered a whole burnt offering for each of them, for Job thought: "Perhaps my children sinned and cursed God in their hearts." Thus did Job regularly behave.[1]

In these verses we learn that Job's children regularly held feasts and that it was Job's custom afterward to offer sacrifices on their behalf in case they might have committed some serious yet inadvertent offense. On the one hand we could infer that the rhetorical role of this vignette is to illustrate that Job is indeed ritually conscientious to a fault. This would serve little purpose if the book is not intending to include ritual offenses or solutions in its purview. But what is the alternative? If we consider what connection this vignette does have in the remainder of the book, we might conclude that this part of the profile is not intended to convey another of Job's strengths but to show a potential vulnerability.

As the book unfolds and Job repeatedly tries to engage a mediator and to confront God in court, he apparently has concluded that God must be petty—visiting the righteous with intense suffering and misfortune for a technicality. Imagine today a policeman pulling someone over and giving him a speeding ticket for going 56 mph in a 55-mph zone when everyone else is going 80 mph. Job at times explicitly accuses God of such picayune enforcement (e.g., Job 7:17-21; 16:7-17).

In light of the posture that Job adopts in his speeches—suggesting that God may be petty and overly exacting in his expectations—we can re-evaluate the rhetorical purpose of Job's customary response in the aftermath of the celebrations of his children. As the text articulates it, there is no offense of his children that is known to Job, nor would his children have consciously committed an outward offense. Job's actions (and fears) are based on unsubstantiated and improbable offenses. His ritual routine therefore suggests that he considers God petty. If this is the case, this part of Job's profile is not complimentary. When God does strike out at Job, it is this assumption of pettiness that guides Job's suspicions about God.

Awareness of this inference about the rhetorical intention behind this vignette is of great importance as the plot unfolds. Job's ritually conscientious custom provides the bridge into the scene in heaven. God's observations about Job focus on the narrator's description in Job 1:1. It is reasonable to consider that the challenger's suggestion is built on the potential implications of Job 1:4-5. If Job harbors a suspicion that God is inclined to be petty, so much so that he engages in these fastidious rituals based on such meager possibilities, one might infer that Job is motivated (not only in his piety, but in his righteousness) by fear of being the target of attack by an unreasonable and capricious deity. If that inference is sustainable, then one might also wonder whether Job also secretly believes that such a god can be, or even needs to be, bought. If Job is motivated to piety because he believes God to be petty, is it not also possible that Job is motivated to righteousness because he believes God's favors are on auction? Such thinking would represent the consistent application of the great symbiosis.

The challenger has reason to believe that Job simply acts within the confines of the great symbiosis. Thus the challenger feels justified in raising the issue before God. This interpretation of Job 1:4-5 therefore offers an explanation of why the challenger questions Job's motivation. The suggestion of the challenger is not an act of malice; it is one of logical inference.

JOB HAS INTEGRITY

Job is far from perfect even in the opening profile, and his response to his suffering is one among a number of ways of thinking that the book eventually rejects. But there is one thing Job gets right, and it is the most important thing for the message that the book requires: Job retains his integrity. The key affirmation that demonstrates this is found in Job's last speech to his friends (Job 27:1-6). The same Hebrew word translated often as *integrity* is used in Job 2:3, 9; 6:29 and 31:6, and words from the same root are used in various sorts of contexts throughout the book. Outside of the book of Job, this noun form occurs only in Proverbs 11:3. The word's connotation is clearly delineated by the various clauses Job uses to describe it in Job 27:4-6, particularly his assertion that he maintains his innocence with no reproach from his conscience.

How would his integrity have been violated or compromised? The challenger asks whether Job serves God for nothing. Integrity would therefore be defined as serving God for nothing. If Job demonstrates that he serves God for nothing, he maintains his integrity. Two external assaults pressure Job to forfeit that integrity. The first is the blatant advice of his wife that he renounce his integrity: "Curse God and die" (Job 2:9). Such a response would demonstrate that Job really only cares about his benefits, not his righteousness.

The second assault is sustained over the three cycles of speeches by his friends. In contradistinction to the course of action taken by his wife, the friends pressure Job to undertake strategies that will conceivably lead to the restoration of his prosperity. Job maintains his innocence and will never admit that they are right (Job 27:5). If Job were to follow the advice of either his wife or his friends, it would demonstrate that he did *not* serve God for nothing; his integrity would be forfeit. Given this focused definition of his integrity, we can see that integrity is not a wide-ranging blanket affirmation that Job is irreproachable in every way. Though it is a qualified exoneration, it is all that is needed for the message of the book.

Before concluding this section, we should briefly address two assessments that may undermine this interpretation. The first comes within the book itself where God affirms that Job spoke "the truth" or "what is right" about God (Job 42:7-8). This has been considered a befuddling statement by readers of the book because just two chapters earlier God had reprimanded Job for calling God's justice into question. If Job did so (and he patently did several times in his speeches—for example, in Job 30:18-23, and see God's charge in Job 40:8), then how can he be congratulated on speaking what was right and true about God?

The key must be found in the particular nuances of the Hebrew word that is used here, *nekonah,* and in the rendering of the preposition in the NIV's translation ("spoken the truth *about* me").[2] With regard to the Hebrew word, we recognize that authors exercise choices when they decide what word to use, and a careful investigation about this word can clarify the subtleties that it conveys. The description of something as *nekonah* indicates that it is logical, sensible or verifiable. As such it may be considered appropriate, truthful or right unless there are mitigating circumstances that overturn it. More importantly, the combination of this Hebrew verb and preposition ("spoken . . . about") consistently throughout the Old Testament means to "speak to" someone who is generally present. Consequently the description *nekonah* would refer to what Job has spoken to God in his previous speech (Job 42:1-6). It would not describe everything Job has said throughout the book. The objection to this view in the past has been that Eliphaz and Job's other friends have not spoken *anything* to God. But it would be more awkward for the text to say, "You did not speak anything at all to me to acknowledge your misconceptions in comparison to the appropriate (*nekonah*) words that Job spoke." It covers this quite nicely instead by saying that they have made no appropriate expressions to God as Job has done. The resulting interpretation is that God does not declare everything Job has said to be right; he rather gives approval to Job's response in Job 42:1-6 and chastises the friends for not being comparably penitent.

The second assessment that may undermine this interpretation is found in James 5:11, where it appears that Job receives a character endorsement. From the start we should be sure that we understand what James is claiming for Job. It is not Job's righteousness, or anything else in the opening profile of Job, that James praises him for. Rather the text praises Job for his perseverance or endurance (or, according to another understanding of the Greek term [*hypomonē*] in the context, his patience, as in the KJV) and therefore reflects on his response to suffering. Job was not patient, which is why most modern translations opt for "perserverance" or an equivalent translation rather than "patience." If, as the KJV and some modern commentators believe, James points to Job's patience, then he is reading the biblical book of Job through the prism of his own time period (represented by the *Testament of Job*). The biblical Job did persevere, remaining steadfast in his claim of innocence, and the Job of the *Testament of Job* was patient. Whichever Job James has in mind, he does not give comprehensive endorsement of Job's character but highlights one specific aspect of his response, and indeed we should also be steadfast (or patient) as we encounter suffering or even persecution.

JOB THE SELF-RIGHTEOUS

We have already identified the flaw in Job's thinking related to his opinion that God is petty and overly exacting in his demands. The other major shortcoming we find in Job is his self-righteousness. We might well object that since Job is indeed righteous, it is difficult for self-righteousness to be a fault. The problem arises, however, when Job's view of his righteousness is so confident that he is ready to denigrate God's justice to maintain it. Just such an accusation is leveled against Job by Elihu (e.g., Job 33:9-12; 34:34-37), but more importantly it is confirmed by God (Job 40:8).

Though Job is suitably chastised by God for this posture, self-righteousness is an important aspect of Job's characterization in the rhetorical strategy of the book because it is this confidence in his own righteousness (above all else) that stands him in good stead as he maintains his integrity and resists the urging of his wife and friends. Though we might personally assess his attitude as arrogant and be shocked at his hubris as he calls God to account, the book is not trying to sort out the strengths and weaknesses of Job's character. From a literary standpoint the primary concern is whether he succeeds as the witness for the defense of God's policies.

FOR FURTHER REFLECTION

1. Summarize the character of Job as presented in the book of Job.

2. Compare and contrast the character of Job as a righteous man with that of Noah and Abraham.

3. Read Job 31 and list all the qualities that make Job a righteous person.

EIGHT

HOW TO ASSESS
JOB'S HUMAN ADVISERS

Up until the divine theophany begins in Job 38, Job interacts with other people who offer him advice about how to deal with his suffering. While his three friends (Eliphaz, Bildad and Zophar) are best known, we also meet his wife and a young man named Elihu along the way. How are we to assess their roles in the book? Let's meet them now, beginning with the three friends.

JOB'S THREE FRIENDS: ELIPHAZ, BILDAD AND ZOPHAR

Job's friends have roles; they are characters in this drama. It is unlikely that the book would present three friends if one could have sufficed for its rhetorical strategy. That is, if all three friends are univocal in their assessment and advice, they serve no differentiated literary purpose. In our understanding the author is too skilled to be wasteful of the characters. Some might object that maybe we should just accept this as historical and say that there *were* three friends who came. While that option remains on the table, we also recognize that even if we accept that the author is preserving historical events, even authors of undeniably historical events make literary choices regarding what to include and what to leave out based on their literary objectives. The author likely portrays the friends as having distinct approaches even though they also serve a unified role. As readers we should seek to be sensitive to both.

Having said that, however, we should exercise caution regarding how we classify the friends. Some have used labels that echo modern philosophical approaches. (One common proposal identifies Eliphaz as a mystic, Bildad as a traditionalist and Zophar as a rationalist.) These modern categories may not be far off the mark in general terms, but we should recognize that rationalism is probably not a viable category for ancient Near Eastern thinking. Alternatively we could suggest that Eliphaz gives most weight to his personal experiences, Bildad relies on the wisdom of the ages and Zophar is most inclined to find understanding in a system of thinking in which everything is black and white. The result of these descriptions does not really differ from the first. The important point is to see that the three friends represent different perspectives, though they all agree on the conclusion that Job is suffering because he is a sinner. They may come at it from different perspectives, but they all represent the view of retribution theology. Thus there is also a sense of piling on in the choice to have three friends, rather than just one, interacting with Job.

It is also important to recognize that the three cycles of speeches differ from one another in their focus. In the first set of speeches, the friends offer advice to Job. They use generalizations peppered with exhortations as they hold out the hope of restoration. In the second cycle, they turn their attention to the fate of the wicked. No hint of commiseration remains as they repeatedly insult and humiliate Job with insinuations. In the third cycle, they turn to direct accusation of Job. Figure 8.1 summarizes the arguments of the various friends through the cycles of their speeches.[1]

Now that we have discussed what differentiates the friends and the dialogue cycles, we can turn our attention to the unified role that they play. First of all, the friends corporately represent the sages of the ancient world. They are the wisest men who can be found, and in that role they offer the cutting-edge philosophy of the day. Whatever answers are available are known to them. In this role they are foils because the book rejects the wisdom that they have to offer as shallow and inadequate, flawed reasoning built on flimsy assumptions. They come as representatives of wisdom and are dismissed as misguided fools.

	Cycle 1: Exhortation and Advice	Cycle 2: Fate of the Wicked	Cycle 3: Accusation
Eliphaz	Appeal to God and admit your offense.	Recognize your guilt by comparing how God treats the wicked to how he is treating you. You have nullified your own piety.	Repent, be restored and go on the lecture circuit.
Job	Stop treating me as guilty. Rather than appeal to God with false humility and trumped-up offenses, I will confront him with demands for vindication.	I need protection from God's attacks and call for an advocate to take up my case.	Look around you! Who can think about self when the world is so out of sync?
Bildad	Take the traditional retribution principle seriously and recognize the inevitable conclusion.	Give up the pretense; the wicked are doomed. You are among those who do not know God.	Face the fact that tradition knows best.
Job	I know the traditions are true, but I am not ready to admit the conclusions are inevitable. Yet I am without recourse.	It is God that has messed up my life, not me. A defender will arise and vindicate me from your insinuations.	God's immense power has brought order to the cosmos but not to my life—I am God's victim and you will be too. Here I stand with only my righteousness to cling to.
Zophar	Devote you heart to God and put away sin.	Your sin is pride, and God has judged you as wicked.	None
Job	You are badly misrepresenting God and me. I hope I can get my hearing and restore my relationship with God before I die.	The system (God's policies) is broken.	None

Figure 8.1. Summary of speeches in the dialogues (Job 4–27)

Second, the friends together play the role of representing, at least in part, the thinking of the ancient Near East. This characterization of them must be immediately qualified by the recognition that they are missing one major element of ancient Near Eastern thinking: they neither consider Job's offenses to be in the realm of ritual negligence nor do they advise ritual strategies for restoration. Aside from that caveat we see that the friends are all interested in helping Job to appease a god who is angry (in their minds undoubtedly and justifiably so) in order that he might be restored to favor and prosperity. They therefore share a common goal and agree on the strategy to achieve it. This appeasement approach to suffering is the common one in the ancient world (discussed above, p. 29). Again, however, the appeasement is not based on some ritual to be performed but rather in confession of wrongs, whether they be real, imagined, hypothetical or comprehensive (i.e., confessing to many wrongs without regard to whether you think you committed them or not).

Beyond this general perspective on a response to suffering (which echoes that of the ancient world), we could further investigate whether they offer the answers that commonly emerge when such matters are discussed in ancient literature. Such answers include the following:

- No sinless child has been born.

- Gods have made people with evil inclinations and prone to suffering.

- Gods are inscrutable since they are inconsistent and unpredictable.

- The purposes of the gods are remote.

It would be very difficult to see any of these answers consistently adopted by the friends. They do not believe that Job could possibly be righteous given the severity of his suffering and the suddenness of his fall. Therefore they can maintain that the retribution principle provides the explanation for Job's circumstances. They do not need to resort to an inscrutable or remote god.

Third and most importantly in the rhetorical strategy of the book, the friends collectively play the role of the challenger's philosophical representatives. That is, through their arguments they are urging Job to a course of action that, should he adopt it, would indicate the challenger was correct about Job's motives for righteous behavior. If Job is willing to confess to sins that he does not believe he has committed in order to appease an angry god and have his prosperity restored (as the friends urge), it would demonstrate that Job is motivated by prosperity rather than by righteousness as the challenger had suspected.

In summary, then, the friends do generally stand as representatives of wisdom in the ancient world, but they do not offer the answers of the ancient world. Rather than firmly embedded cultural characters, they are literary characters with a literary role. They are not included in order to provide instruction in how *not* to give counsel or comfort. They are not role models; they are role players.

ELIHU'S SURPRISING APPEARANCE

During the lengthy three-cycle dispute between Job and his three friends, there is no mention of any other people, no individual or gathered crowd. Thus we are surprised that a young man named Elihu makes his presence known in Job 32–37. He states that he has been silent as he deferred to those older than he is, but now he is emboldened based on his belief that he is filled with the spirit (Job 32:18).

Elihu plays an entirely different role from that of the three friends. The dialogues in Job 4–27 press the case of the challenger, who has wondered whether Job is motivated by righteousness alone or by what he stands to gain, thereby suggesting that it is not good policy for righteous people to prosper. The dialogues exert significant pressure on Job in order to flush out what his true motives are. He withstands the pressure of the friends and thus demonstrates that his righteousness has not been motivated by potential material benefits. The challenger's contention is rebutted by the end of the dialogues, but Job's challenge to God's policies remains unaddressed. Job's position is that it is not good policy for God to allow righteous people to suffer. The discourse section of the book (Job 29–41) is going to address that, and here is where we encounter Elihu.

Elihu does not advise Job to confess to sins of the past (sins of which no one is aware). He is not involved in the discussion of Job's motives for being righteous. While the friends could only deduce that Job must have committed vile sins (inferred from his suffering), Elihu has a very specific accusation to make. His accusation does not identify something in the past (prior to Job's fall) or something that is hidden. Elihu accuses Job of self-righteousness so extreme that even God's character is impugned before it.

Elihu's advice to Job is that he should abandon his self-righteousness. Just as the first part of the book provided the answer concerning Job's motivation, this part offers reflections on how Job, an ostensibly righteous man, can be subject to suffering. To understand the role of Elihu, we first need to consider Job's discourse in Job 29–31. In Job's speech he documented his fall (Job 29, his prosperity; Job 30, his deplorable current circumstances) and then concluded with an oath of innocence. In that oath he declared his innocence across a wide spectrum of behaviors. This represented a strategy to demonstrate that he is indeed a righteous person and not a wicked one. By swearing an oath that he did not engage in these wicked practices, Job obligates God to act in punishment if the oath is false. God's silence would be tacit admission that Job is righteous, thereby highlighting in sharp relief the problem of righteous people suffering.

Elihu then steps in to present a contrasting position because from his perspective Job is not righteous. Again, note that here the discussion has turned from what motivated Job's righteousness to whether Job *is* righteous. God has appeared to treat him as if he were not, so the oath strategy is adopted. Elihu claims that Job's responses to suffering mark him as lacking in the humility that characterizes true righteousness.

Elihu is the only one in the book who offers a specific accusation pertaining to a specific breach in Job's righteous façade. He contends that Job's self-righteous defense of himself is serious enough to justify punitive action against him. His logic departs from the standard way of thinking, in which offense is committed and judgment is then carried out. The Elihu variation is that judgment may precede offense since it can have the purpose of drawing out the offensive behavior. In this case, Job's offensive self-righteousness, so strident that it undermines the justice of God, was not evident until he began to suffer. Therefore the suffering was necessary in order to reveal the problem.

In this way Elihu's role in the second part of the book parallels the role of the challenger by proposing an alternate way to view Job's righteousness. The challenger questioned Job's motives; Elihu questions Job's righteousness. If this is so, Elihu is not the one who is challenging God's policies (it is Job who does that). Elihu is instead suggesting that a modified form of the retribution principle (not just remedial) can be maintained in Job's case, and therefore the appropriateness of God's policies is not suspect. God is going to agree with Elihu that Job's self-righteousness exceeds acceptable levels, but he is not going to accept Elihu's belief that he has justified Job's suffering and thereby validated a modified retribution principle as an explanation of why righteous people suffer. Though Elihu defends God's policies, he does so from a flawed foundation. When we finally arrive at Yahweh's speeches, we will find that Job's motives have been vindicated and Job's righteousness affirmed (though his self-righteousness is condemned), but God's policies have yet to be understood.

JOB'S WIFE, AN AGENT OF THE CHALLENGER

No discussion of Job's advisers could be complete without some mention of his wife. Her role is minor, so we have left her to last, though she is the first to make an appearance. When she speaks up Job has already suffered both stages of his affliction (his prosperity and his health). His response to the first round had been that Yahweh is the one who gives good gifts, so if he takes away, who should complain? His name should be blessed (Job 1:21). Job's wife registers her advice in the aftermath of the second round, telling Job to relinquish his integrity, to "curse God and die" (Job 2:9). Job's second response follows and is similar to his first. Referring to her as a "foolish woman" (Job 2:10), he embraces the perspective that if we accept that which is good from God's hand, we should also be willing to accept trouble.

The rhetorical role of Job's wife is as obvious as her suggestion is blatantly scandalous. She serves as an instrument of the challenger's expectations just as the friends do. Once again the challenger is proven correct if Job follows his wife's advice. The challenger said that Job would curse God to his face, and that is precisely what Job's wife advises him to do. If Job does so, his motives will be shown to be flawed—he is only committed to being righteous if he is receiving benefits for doing so.

We need to pause here briefly for an examination of the concept of cursing God. What is striking, and not obvious from English translations, is that every place in Job 1–2 where the text talks about "cursing" God (Job 1:5, 11; 2:5, 9), the Hebrew word that is used (*barak*) means "bless" (translated that way in Job 1:10, 21). The common explanation is that when the direct object of the verb was God, there was some reluctance to actually use the verb that means "curse." The avoidance of potentially offensive words and constructions is called euphemism. This use of euphemism produces an odd juxtaposition since the challenger claims that Job will *barak* God to his face (meaning "curse," Job 1:11). Yet, apparently in contrast, Job *barak*s God (meaning "bless," [NIV "praise"] Job 1:21).

Some have wondered whether Job's wife has been misunderstood. Was she just telling Job that, though he continues to bless God, he is apparently going to die anyway? Grammatically and logically this may have been a possible understanding, but it is refuted contextually by the fact that Job responds to her suggestion by labeling her as a "foolish" woman. She serves no rhetorical role if she just makes a passing comment. The traditional way of interpreting her statement is the only one that makes sense in the rhetorical development.

As we have seen, then, all these characters play their respective roles as the author's strategy develops. We evaluate them as characters in the literature rather than as people we might meet (whether they existed and said these things or not).

FOR FURTHER REFLECTION

1. Write a short paragraph describing the role played in the book of Job by each of Job's human participants: the three friends, Elihu and Job's wife.

2. Read a speech from each of the three friends and summarize their arguments against Job. Are they similar or different? In what way?

3. Describe how Elihu's approach to Job differs from that of the three friends.

NINE

WHO IS JOB'S ADVOCATE?

The advocate in Job is one who, like Godot in *Waiting for Godot*, never actually makes an appearance. Having said that, the book is not without characters who aspire to that role (Elihu) or who serve part of that function (the challenger).

THE LEXICAL PROFILE OF THE ADVOCATE

We have chosen to use the term *advocate* in this section (though others could have been easily chosen) for the fact is that several different Hebrew words are used to describe this character (he could hardly be called an individual) in the book, primarily in Job 16:18-21. A full listing would include[1]

- Cry (*za'aqah*),[2] Job 16:18
- Witness (*'ed*), Job 16:19
- Advocate (*sahed*), Job 16:19
- Intercessor (*melits*), Job 16:20; 33:23 (NIV "messenger")
- Redeemer (*go'el*), Job 19:25
- One who pleads (*yokakh/mokiakh*), Job 9:33 (NIV "someone to mediate"); 16:21

As we examine the terms individually, we find that "witness" (*'ed*) and "arbitrator" (*yokakh/mokiakh*) function specifically in the legal realm. "Advocate" (*sahed*) occurs only here, but its usage in other related Semitic languages indicates its legal function.[3] "Intercessor" (*melits*) occurs four other times and, though its contexts vary, always refers to someone who speaks on behalf of another ("interpreter," Gen 42:23; "envoys," 2 Chron 32:31; "spokesmen," most likely prophets and priests, Is 43:27 [NIV "those I sent to teach you"]).

WHAT KIND OF ADVOCATE DOES JOB WANT?

Particularly in the first round of speeches, Job seeks an opportunity to face God in court for the purpose of having the charges against him made public. In Job's mind this would give him the opportunity to refute the charges and claim his innocence. This desire is most pronounced in his reply to Zophar in Job 13. There, however, even as he pleads for this chance, he fears that God will exploit the situation and simply overwhelm him with majestic intimidation. In light of this exigency, Job adopts an alternative path in which some sort of mediator advocates on his behalf in the divine court. Job invokes an intercessor primarily in his reply to Eliphaz in the second cycle of speeches (Job 16), though the concept is briefly considered in his first response to Bildad (Job 9:33-35).

What is the nature of this mediator or advocate that Job expects? Clines's view is distinctive as he proposes that the advocate is merely a personification of Job's cry.[4] More commonly, interpreters have concluded that the mediator is God himself.[5] The disadvantage of this view is clear enough: one of the parties involved in the dispute cannot easily serve as mediator if he is to be effective. Job suspects God of inappropriate acts against him, so justice could hardly be expected if God himself is the mediator.

Two other possibilities have been regularly considered. A third party could theoretically be found among either human relatives or friends or, alternatively, among heavenly beings, presumably in the divine council (the "sons of God"). In either case the individual would represent Job in court, testify on his behalf and advocate for his innocence. Ideally, as a result God would be called to accountability.

If the mediator role is to be played by a human being, it would logically be a relative (the typical role of the *go'el* in Israelite society) or, in a less likely scenario, a friend ("a friend who sticks closer than a brother," Prov 18:24).[6] Job's relatives have abandoned him (Job 19:13-14; interesting that they come back out of the woodwork once he has been restored, Job 42:11), and any other friend who remains and has confidence in him would have no access to the heavenly court. Elihu appears to offer himself as a mediator.[7] Yet as Elihu unfolds his proposal and describes the role he expects to play, he seems to describe an arbitrator serving both sides rather than a mediator working on Job's behalf. Based on his insight into Job's situation, Elihu is going to offer advice to Job that he believes will spare Job's life (Job 33:32). In Elihu's mind, then, Job is not righteous but can take a path that will lead to reconciliation. Elihu anticipates that he can negotiate a settlement suitable to both parties (Job 33:25-27). Consequently we can see that though Elihu projects himself into this role, he is not the sort of mediator that Job wants nor the sort that can provide solutions within the context of the book.

The only option left is that Job requests and expects a mediator or advocate to be a heavenly being arising from within the heavenly court—some being who will call God to accountability. Interestingly, Elihu suggests such a possibility when he says to Job,

> Yet if there is an angel at their side,
> > a messenger, one out of a thousand,
> > sent to tell them how to be upright,
> and he is gracious to that person and says to God,
> > "Spare them from going down to the pit." (Job 33:23-24)

However, for Job the irony is palpable. The only heavenly being speaking about Job is the challenger in Job 1–2, and his communication about Job is what precipitated the predicament of the book of Job—a righteous person suffering.[8]

Early in the dialogues Eliphaz had dismissed the idea of a mediator from the divine court (Job 5:1), and in his third speech (Job 22:2-3) he suggests that even if such a mediator came to his aid, Job might not be well served by that approach. Eliphaz's comments in Job 22:2-3 are extremely difficult to translate. On the basis of a thorough analysis of the grammar and syntax of the verses, we would offer the following translation:[9]

> Can a wise mediator do any good for a human being [serving] on
>   behalf of God?
>   Can such a mediator bring a human any benefit?
> Will God respond favorably when you justify yourself?
>   Will there be a gain when you give full account of your ways?

Eliphaz's point is a valid one: even should the mediator succeed and successfully press the suit, it would ultimately be counterproductive to prove that God is wrong. Successful intervention is highly unlikely and would be detrimental.

We find then that though Job ardently desires some sort of advocate or mediator to come to his aid, one has already been involved (the challenger), and he is unlikely to procure another. Even if he did he could not win. If by some fluke he did win, the result would be devastating. If Job is right about God and, with the help of a mediator, forces God to give an explanation (and there is not a logical one), then God is shown to be unworthy of worship. If Job uses this strategy and "wins," God loses.

In conclusion, a mediator will not do any good. Having a mediator is not the solution to Job's situation, nor is it the pathway to provide answers to the questions the book is addressing. A mediator will not bring a resolution to our suffering or provide a way of thinking about God when life goes wrong. It is not uncommon that people who are suffering want to make their case before God, but the book rejects this option as an acceptable resolution. We must look elsewhere.

IS JESUS THE ADVOCATE?

As Christians reading this book, should we assume the mediator, particularly the *go'el* of Job 19:25, to be Jesus?[10] It is self-evident that neither Job nor the author of the book has Jesus in mind as the "redeemer" in Job 19:25. The bigger question is whether Job expresses the need for someone like Jesus. That is, is the role of *go'el* one that Job hopes for and that only Jesus can fill? If we turn to the New Testament, we will not find any hint that those authors made a connection between Job's *go'el* and the role of Jesus. Certainly Jesus is our Redeemer and arguably also then serves in the role of *go'el*. The most important point to note, however, is that Job is looking for someone to demonstrate that he is righteous—innocent of the putative crimes. He is not looking for someone who will take the punishment for his offenses and thus justify him. Job is looking for vindication, not justification. Vindication is emphatically *not* something that Jesus provides. By this reasoning Job is expecting someone to play a role that is the polar opposite of that which is played by Jesus. This being the case, viewing Jesus as the *go'el* in Job distorts the interpretation of the book and runs against the grain of Job's hope. Jesus is not the answer to the problems posed in the book of Job, though he *is* the answer to the larger problem of sin and the brokenness of the world. The death and the resurrection of Jesus mediate for our sin but do not explain why there is suffering in the world or how we should think about God when life goes wrong.

FOR FURTHER REFLECTION

1. Why does Job want to take God to court?

2. What role does Job want an advocate to play?

3. Does Job ever find an advocate?

4. Would it have done him any good to find one?

TEN

BEHEMOTH AND LEVIATHAN, THE MOST POWERFUL CREATURES IMAGINABLE

The last characters to consider in the book of Job are the creatures Behemoth and Leviathan. In Yahweh's speeches, discussion of these creatures comes after Job has made his first response (Job 40:4-5), in which he has acknowledged his inability to answer God's questions. Yahweh's points in Job 38–39 address the complexity of the world and Job's ignorance of the way that the world works. This point is significant because Job and his friends had confidently formulated a theory that reduced the operations of the world to a single, simple proposition—the retribution principle.

WHAT ARE THESE CREATURES?

After this first response by Job, Yahweh presses his case further. He reprimands Job for having considered his own righteousness as a basis for questioning God's justice (Job 40:8) and rhetorically challenges Job's ability to impose justice on the world (Job 40:10-13). This harsh rhetoric sets the scene for the introduction of Behemoth and Leviathan. They do not serve the same rhetorical role as the previous animals mentioned (wild ox, ostrich, etc., Job 38–39). The discussion no longer concerns Job's simplistic ignorance nor the suggestion that Job don the mantle of divinity and run the world. Instead Yahweh now turns to these two creatures to address the question of what Job's posture and attitude ought to be. These two "characters" therefore offer the path by which the answers in the book are provided.

Much ink has been spilled concerning the identification of these two creatures. Most commonly they are identified as known zoological species. The placement of Behemoth among the lotus plants in the river (Job 40:21-24) has conveniently suggested the hippopotamus, a creature of mythical proportions that was feared and hunted in Egypt. The described habitat would make that reasonable enough, but the description of the tail as "like a cedar" (Job 40:17) eliminates that possibility. In similar fashion, Leviathan may well share some physical features with the Nile crocodile, but other features refute that option: crocodiles neither breathe fire (Job 41:18-21) nor have multiple heads (Ps 74:14).[1] And besides these points, the hippopotamus and the crocodile are animals that humans can kill or control, so if they are such animals, then God's argument of his sole ability to control them does not have much punch.

These complications have led others to suspect that Behemoth and Leviathan are creatures that are now extinct: dinosaurs such as Brontosaurus or Tyrannosaurus. Aside from the fact that these suggestions come from those who believe that dinosaurs coexisted with humans, we also find that the descriptions do not match any known dinosaurs. It would be quite a stretch to imagine a Brontosaurus being concealed among the reeds, and no dinosaur is known to have breathed fire and to have had multiple heads.

Instead we should look to the literature from the ancient world to identify these creatures. In that context it is more likely that the hippopotamus and crocodile might be considered reminiscent of Behemoth and Leviathan, perhaps even their lesser spawn in some sense. Behemoth and Leviathan would then be quintessential creatures whose abstract characteristics are shared by the known animals. This would put Behemoth and Leviathan in the category of chaos creatures or, perhaps preferably, anti-cosmos creatures. Such creatures are part of the ordered world but serve as agents of non-order by virtue of their mindless nature. They are not morally evil, but they can do serious harm. They are not enemies of God, but they can wreak havoc among humans. In other words Behemoth (which is the plural of the word for "cattle") means the most potent land animal imaginable, while Leviathan would be the most potent sea creature imaginable.

POSSIBLE ANCIENT NEAR EASTERN BACKGROUNDS

Besides fitting into this general category of anti-cosmos creatures in ancient Near Eastern thinking, these creatures have also at times been connected with known iconography. Figurines and reliefs from Mesopotamia portray a human-headed bison that interpreters have associated with Behemoth. Leviathan is mentioned in Ugaritic texts (*Litan*) and has been associated with seals and engravings that portray a seven-headed dragon in battle with a heroic figure. While these associations are not outside the realm of possibility, we cannot depend on them and so set them aside.

Other interpreters have gone so far as to associate Behemoth and Leviathan with specific creatures mentioned in West Semitic (Ugaritic) mythological pieces—characters in narratives. Collins associates them with Mot and Yamm,[2] while Day prefers to identify Behemoth with El's calf, Atik (*Arš*), and Leviathan with the Ugaritic mythological sea dragon, Litan.[3] The evidence is insufficient to make a confident connection between Behemoth and Leviathan on the one hand and specific myths on the other. Yet one might well locate these two creatures in Job at the intersection of the world of nature with the world of myth. The point is that these creatures would have been recognizable to the ancient audience.

JOB MUST EMULATE BEHEMOTH AND THINK ABOUT GOD LIKE HE THINKS ABOUT LEVIATHAN

In the end it is not as important to arrive at a confident identification of these two creatures as it is to recognize how the author of the book uses them. Whatever else they may be, they are literary characters here in Job, and the author makes use of them for a rhetorical purpose. It is our task as interpreters to discern what that purpose is. To achieve this we must attend very carefully to what the author actually says about them.

As the speech shifts from Yahweh's reprimand of Job back to discussion of what God does (note "I made" in Job 40:15), we have to set the speech in the context of previous significant points in the book. In Job's lament he spoke of those who were ready to take on Leviathan (Job 3:8), and in Job's first response to Eliphaz he asked why God was treating him as if he were a chaos creature (Job 7:12, using *tannin*, the same Hebrew word as in Gen 1:21 [NIV "great creatures of the sea"]) by keeping him under guard. Gods in the ancient Near East were known to keep partially domesticated chaos creatures on leash. Job goes even further in his discourse later in the book when he suggests that God himself is acting like a chaos creature (Job 30:15-23).[4]

With these contexts in mind, it is interesting that Yahweh picks two chaos creatures for this part of the discussion and in a way acknowledges the charges Job had made, but with a twist: God is not treating Job as if he were a chaos creature as much as he asks Job to step into the role of Behemoth. Likewise God is not acting like a chaos creature; instead he is far superior to Leviathan and should be recognized as such. These points need to be unpacked carefully as we proceed.

To begin, Job had emphasized the uncontrolled, anti-cosmos aspect of chaos creatures while Yahweh makes his point by considering them part of the ordered world. This is often how chaos creatures are treated in the biblical text, as is evident in passages such as Genesis 1:21, where they are part of the ordered world, and Psalm 104:26, where they are portrayed as passive, not threatening. These creatures are on the periphery of the ordered world—one foot out, one foot in. Just as the sea is the realm of non-order yet is controlled by God with its boundaries set, these creatures are not domesticated in any sense. This realm is populated by liminal creatures that have been seen, such as the coyote, owl, ostrich and hyena, as well as fearsome beasts only seen in the eyes of imagination. This latter group is not strictly zoological. They have been created by God, but they represent the potential for continuing non-order, like the thorns and thistles in the less ordered realm outside the garden.

Next we must observe very carefully what is said and not said about these creatures. It is immediately obvious that God's comments are not directed toward Job's righteousness nor his own justice. God defends neither in this speech. After the description of Behemoth, the only point made concerns the creature's stability in surging waters (Job 40:23). Behemoth is not righteous, and Leviathan is not just. Behemoth cannot be moved, and Leviathan cannot be challenged. Furthermore, God does not defeat them or harness them to show his superiority over them. These two creatures are used as illustrations from which humans should learn some important lessons. Humans should respond to raging rivers with security and trust (as Behemoth does) and should not think that they can domesticate or challenge God (since they cannot challenge or domesticate Leviathan, who is inferior to God).

In Job 40:11, Yahweh challenges Job to "look at all who are proud [*ge'eh*] and bring them low." Using a different root, but one that sounds quite similar, Job 41:34 identifies Leviathan as the one who "looks down on all that are haughty." In fact, Leviathan is said to be king over this sort of person. Job is therefore seen as incapable of taking on the role of Leviathan. But more importantly Job is incapable of overthrowing or domesticating Leviathan. The detailed comparison below draws out these points.

Job is explicitly compared to Behemoth at the initial introduction to the beast (Job 40:15).[5] Job, like Behemoth, is the first of God's works (cf. Job 15:7) and withstands all turbulence. God brings his sword against Job (Job 40:19), and by a snare he penetrates Job's anger (Job 40:24). Yahweh does not speak of Job doing anything *to* Behemoth, but when the discussion switches to Leviathan, the first eight verses use the second person. This switch suggests that Leviathan is to be compared to Yahweh (Job 41:3, 10-11, 34)[6]—he won't beg you for mercy and won't speak with gentle words; you cannot put him on a leash, subdue him or rouse him. These all discuss what *Job* cannot do to Leviathan, and they are also things that Job must learn he cannot do to Yahweh. The following summary identifies how Yahweh presents Behemoth as an illustration for Job to emulate and Leviathan as an illustration of how Job should think about Yahweh.[7]

Behemoth.

- Begins with comparison to Job—"along with you,"[8] Job 40:15
- Content and well-fed (as you have been), Job 40:15
- Made strong (as I made you), Job 40:16-18

- Ranks first among its kind (as you do), Job 40:19

- Cared for (as you were), Job 40:20

- Sheltered (as you were), Job 40:21-22

- Not alarmed by a raging river (as you should not be), Job 40:23

- Trusts and is secure (as you should be), Job 40:23

- Cannot be captured or trapped (to which you should also be invulnerable), Job 40:24

- Nose (i.e., anger) cannot be "pierced" (difficult word—sometimes means "named," "designated" or "penetrated") (to which you should also be invulnerable), Job 40:24

Note that the text does not say what Job can or cannot do with regard to Behemoth, or what God does with Behemoth.

Leviathan. The text switches immediately to "you," focusing on what Job cannot do to Leviathan. That is, if you can't do this to Leviathan, why do you expect to do it to me? Likewise this passage never talks about what God does to Leviathan (e.g., his control of him or defeat of him).[9]

- Cannot be controlled (neither can Yahweh), Job 41:1-2

- Will not submit or beg for mercy (neither will Yahweh), Job 41:3-6

- Cannot be wounded or subdued; hopeless to struggle against him (same is true of Yahweh), Job 41:7-9

- Outright comparison: can't rouse him, so who can "stand against me?" Job 41:10

- No one (including you, Job) has a claim against *me*, Job 41:11

- Cannot force his mouth open to receive a bridle (so Yahweh cannot be controlled or domesticated), Job 41:12-18

- Dangerous when riled (as is Yahweh), Job 41:19-25

- Invulnerable (as is Yahweh), Job 41:26-32

- No creature is his equal (nor is Job Leviathan's equal, let alone Yahweh's equal), Job 41:33

- Dominates all who are proud (Job 41:34; cf. Job 40:11-14, where the section was introduced); Job cannot humble the proud (Job 40:11-12), nor can he subdue the king over the proud (41:34); God is also king of the proud in the sense that he rules over them (Job 41:34)

This interpretation differs significantly from others that have been offered by other interpreters. These creatures are not portrayed as the embodiment of cosmic evil.[10] Neither creature is described as evil, and neither creature represents Satan. Nor do they take up the role or the position of the challenger from the early chapters. Furthermore these creatures are not described in such a way that they can serve as evidence of God's ability to subdue threats to the ordered world and bring cosmic justice. No reference to God subduing them can be found here, and cosmic justice is neither hanging in the balance nor the result of what Yahweh is said to do here. The book does not assert that God brings justice either to the cosmos as a whole or to human experience.

Job needs to find stability in rough waters, and he needs to have more respect for Yahweh. This is the message of the book and therefore is appropriately found in Yahweh's last speech. Job's second response (Job 42:2-6) shows that he understands the points Yahweh is making. He acknowledges that he had been presumptuous in what he thought he knew. He recants and submits.

FOR FURTHER REFLECTION

1. Behemoth and Leviathan have been identified as animals of some sort, even as dinosaurs by some, but this chapter has argued that they are chaos monsters. What are the strengths and weaknesses of these views? What do you think and why?

2. In what way is Job to emulate Behemoth?

3. How does the description of Leviathan help Job think about Yahweh?

3

THE THEOLOGICAL
MESSAGE OF THE
BOOK OF JOB

■ ■ ■

ELEVEN

THE RETRIBUTION PRINCIPLE
AND THEODICY IN JOB

The retribution principle articulates one of the basic beliefs of human beings in most cultures in most periods of time—at least those who believe in gods of some sort.[1] The retribution principle is, simply stated, *the righteous will prosper and the wicked will suffer.* The oft-appended corollary is that if someone suffers, they are wicked, and if someone prospers, they are righteous. In this formulation all the major words are being used to point to larger categories:

- *Righteous* refers to behavior that pleases God and brings his favor. In some cultures this is found in moral behavior, while in others, in ritually meticulous performance. In some cultures (like ancient Israel), it includes both. It is not an absolute quality (comparable to the righteousness of God) but a relative standard.

- *Prosper* refers to anything perceived to be a blessing or benefit in one's experience. It includes material prosperity, many children and grandchildren, and good health and success in one's endeavors (for Israel, think of humanity's state in the Garden of Eden or, in a post-fall situation, the blessings of the covenant [for instance, see Deut 27–28]). The presence of prosperity often also results in high social standing and respect from others.

- *Wicked* is used in this formula to identify behavior that is displeasing to God or unacceptable in society, or both. It can describe failure to behave in certain ways or failure to participate in necessary rituals.

- *Suffer* covers the general category of negative experiences from crop failure and ill health (of oneself or one's family) to any negative set of circumstances (bad luck, nothing working out right, people taking advantage or threatening). Many of the laments in the Psalms identify these sorts of situations as do the curses of the covenant as enumerated in Deuteronomy 27–28.

It is common for people to believe that their circumstances somehow indicate whether they are in favor or out of favor with God/the gods and signal that they have done something to bring about these circumstances. The Israelites in the Old Testament were no different, and we find similar expectations among the people of the ancient Near East. This belief is at the core of the wisdom literature from the ancient Near East that explores cases of ostensibly righteous, innocent or upright people experiencing difficulties. It is at the core of the book of Job as it represents the basic belief of both Job and his friends. It frames their expectations and stands as the foundation of how the world operates in the economy of a just God.

Even among Christians today it is common to encounter the belief that if someone is doing well in life, he or she must be doing something right—pleasing God and gaining his favor. Inversely, people quickly jump to the conclusion that if life takes a bad turn, there must be a reason. Whether individuals are assessing their own experiences or observing someone else's tragedies, they deduce that some wrong behavior is at the root of any misfortune. Such opinions are comforting because this understanding gives people a sense of control over their lives.

This way of thinking demonstrates a corollary to the retribution principle as mentioned above. If "the righteous will prosper and the wicked suffer" is considered true, it is a small step to jump to the converse: if someone is prospering, they must be righteous; someone who is suffering must be wicked. We can see that in the book of Job all the human characters have drawn this conclusion: Job's dramatic change of circumstances and the depth of his suffering signal that something is desperately wrong in Job's behavior.

The book of Job, then, has placed the retribution principle under the microscope. We have already proposed (p. 14) that the policies of God are on trial, and the retribution principle is the targeted policy. The challenger claims that the retribution principle is detrimental to the development of true righteousness because it sets up an ulterior motive: the anticipation of gain. Job claims that if the retribution principle is not enforced, God's justice becomes suspect.

We therefore need to investigate the theological and biblical merits of the retribution principle. The retribution principle was an attempt to understand, articulate, justify and systematize the logic of God's interaction in the world. The fact that human experience often seemed to deny the tenets of the retribution principle required that the principle be qualified or nuanced in order to be employed realistically in the philosophical/theological discussion. How can God be just if he does not punish the wicked? In order to answer this question, the retribution principle was frequently under discussion in Israelite theodicy, driven particularly by the context of ethical monotheism. Theodicy is understood as the defense of God's justice in a world where suffering exists, though in more modern terms the conversation has grown into a philosophical discussion concerning the origin of evil. The retribution principle does not of necessity operate in the context of theodicy, but because of Israel's theological commitments, this tendency can be observed in the Old Testament. We will return to consideration of the relationship between retribution principle and theodicy after examining the status of the principle in the ancient Near East.

RETRIBUTION PRINCIPLE IN THE ANCIENT NEAR EAST

The literature of the ancient Near East continually demonstrates that people believed that the administration of justice in the human world was a concern and a responsibility of the gods. It was, for example, considered the principal jurisdiction of the Babylonian god Shamash to administer justice. Thus Hammurabi reports to Shamash with his legal

collection. The questions that swirl around the retribution principle lose
their philosophical urgency in the ancient world because injustice in the
world was often blamed not on the gods but on demons and humans. In
Mesopotamian thinking, evil was built into the cosmos by means of the
"control attributes" (Sumerian ME) that are woven into the fabric of the
cosmos, but even those had not been established by the gods. Since evil
existed outside the jurisdiction of the gods, divine administration of
justice did not necessarily eliminate suffering. Some misfortune came
about simply because of how the world was. In both Egyptian and Mesopotamian thinking, the gods were not considered responsible for evil in
the world, and therefore the presence or experience of evil did not have
to be resolved in reference to the justice of the gods (this in contrast to
Israel, where nothing existed outside the jurisdiction of God's sovereignty). In the Sumerian Lament over the Destruction of Ur, the city is
destroyed not as an act of justice or injustice but because it was time for
kingship to be passed on. Likewise with regard to individuals, suffering
could sometimes just be one's lot in life for the present. Personal misfortune could also be attributed to an action offending the gods, even if
the offense was committed innocently. In such cases the gods were not
unjust; they simply were not very forthcoming about communicating
their expectations.

Though Mesopotamians did not seek to defend the justice of the gods,
they still believed in the retribution principle. Since they lacked revelation
of what the deities required, the people believed offense to the gods was
unavoidable and thus sin was pervasive. Consequently no one could claim
to be innocent.[2] But if worshipers had been ritually conscientious, they
expected that the god they worshiped would protect them. This expectation was based not on the belief that the god was just, only that he or
she was sensible. The gods needed what humans provided, and they in
return were capable in most circumstances of providing protection. This
is the great symbiosis that we discussed earlier (pp. 26-28). The offenses
committed against the gods in a large majority of cases constituted failure
to provide what the gods needed or violation of that which was sacred.
The deity naturally responded with anger, disdain or neglect, leaving the

individual vulnerable. The system worked this way not because the gods were just but because they were needy, and the retribution principle remained intact.

In this sense, though people of Mesopotamia might believe that the gods did indeed punish those who earned their wrath, this conviction could not offer an explanation for all suffering. Those who suffered were not assumed to be wicked since in the ancient Near Eastern worldview much of the suffering that people experienced was not orchestrated by the gods but was possible because of the inattention of the gods or simply because of a course of circumstances or the nature of the world. Even if the gods abandoned a person because of some offense, they were not responsible for the ensuing evil—they simply did nothing to prevent it. They had withdrawn their favor and protection.

In Egyptian thinking the retribution principle represented one aspect involved in the establishment of *ma'at*, which was the ultimate goal of the gods and therefore of those who exercised authority on behalf of the gods in the human realm. This connection between retribution principle and *ma'at* is inherent in Jan Assmann's definition of *ma'at*: "the principle that forms individuals into communities and that gives their actions meaning and direction by ensuring that good is rewarded and evil punished."[3] So defined, he considers *ma'at* to represent the totality of all social norms. If *ma'at* is to be preserved and attained, positive behavior should be recognized and recompensed while negative behavior should be punished. This is rooted not in divine attributes (e.g., justice) but in divine goals (pursuit of *ma'at*).

In conclusion, in the ancient Near East the gods had a level of responsibility to see that good and right prevailed, not because they were compelled by their character or attributes, but because they had the power to exercise such influence and it worked to their advantage to do so. The retribution principle was understood as a logical syllogism in a context where gods expected their needs to be met and had the power to punish or recompense accordingly. In Mesopotamia the most natural matrix for retribution-principle thinking was in the realm of ritual, whereas in Egypt it was one of the primary mechanisms in the establishment of *ma'at*.

RETRIBUTION PRINCIPLE AND THEODICY

As mentioned earlier, theodicy in its modern philosophical and existential guise concerns the origin and nature of suffering and evil. In theology proper (whether mythological, broadly metaphysical or that of ethical monotheism), the philosophical question naturally focuses its attention on the divine role in suffering and relationship to evil. The retribution principle progresses from philosophy to pragmatism in trying to understand and formulate how deity acts in the world. The extent to which deity can theoretically be considered responsible for evil is what draws theodicy and retribution principle together in a theological conundrum. The previous section indicated that the gods in the ancient Near East were in part relieved of responsibility because their role in the origin of evil was limited and because they were often only indirectly considered the cause of suffering. This understanding of the role of deity, along with ambivalence regarding whether the gods were inherently just, nearly eliminates theodicy from the discussion. Though people continued to have deep concerns over how deity acted in the world, and therefore their interests in the retribution principle remained robust and vital, the principle could not be employed in theodicy. Given these considerations we would conclude that *theodicy* is a misnomer when applied to the ancient Near East: the origins of evil were impersonal and the gods were not just, nor did they take ethical responsibility for suffering.

In Israel the absence of any source of divine authority other than Yahweh limited the philosophical possibilities regarding the origin of evil and the source of suffering (1 Sam 2:6; Job 2:10; Eccl 7:14; Is 45:7). No supernatural power alongside Yahweh or outside of Yahweh's sphere of power existed. At the same time, Yahweh was considered powerful, good and just. Thus one might say that the theodicy question bloomed in Israel, and in this hothouse of theological tension, the retribution principle provided the traditional explanation despite its obvious inconsistencies in accounting for human experience. As we tour the wisdom literature's treatment of the retribution principle below, we will see the tension between retribution principle as theodicy and retribution principle as theology. The affirmations of the retribution principle in the text are intended to be theological in nature and serve well in that capacity. In contrast, the Israelites were inclined to try to wield that theology in service to theodicy, a role for which it was singularly unsuitable. The role of the book of Job is to perform the radical surgery that separates theology from theodicy, contending that in the end Yahweh's justice must be taken on faith rather than worked out philosophically. He does not need to be defended; he wants to be trusted. The entire constellation of God's attributes is at work in a complex, coordinated manner. Justice is part of that constellation but does not trump all other attributes. Thus the retribution principle cannot serve the purposes of theodicy.

RESOLVING TENSIONS BETWEEN THE RETRIBUTION PRINCIPLE AND EXPERIENCE

Having dealt with the relationship between the retribution principle and the character and activities of deity, we now turn our attention to the relationship between the retribution principle and human experience. General belief in the retribution principle created certain tensions that needed to be resolved in the face of experiences that did not conform to the principle. Resolution of these tensions could potentially assume a number of different configurations.

Qualification regarding the nature of deity. In this approach either deity is not just, the quality of divine justice differs from human perception or deity has simply not given enough information to allow individuals to know what earns his favor or wrath. We have already encountered this latter option in the ancient Near East, where revelation was scant and obligations to deity were often seen in cultic terms. When such was the case, a ritual resolution of suffering was sought by trying to appease a deity who was angry for unknown reasons. This general inclination is observable in the argument of Job's three friends in the dialogue section of the book. The qualification is that sometimes people suffer not because they are wicked but because they are ignorant of their offense, and the retribution principle is retained.

Qualification regarding the purpose of suffering. Suffering in this approach is not simply punishment from a just God—it may have an educational purpose (the explanation emphasized by Elihu in Job 32–37 and stated by Eliphaz in Job 5:17-22), or it may be focused on some spiritual benefit (the position adopted in the New Testament where Christian suffering is seen as sharing in the suffering of Christ). The qualification is that sometimes people suffer because, as uncomfortable as it is, they stand to benefit from it. One form of this is the conviction that suffering builds character. This may represent a departure from the retribution principle formula, as in the Christian context, but can still include an aspect of the retribution principle as it does in Elihu's and Eliphaz's position. Elihu maintained that Job's suffering was still punishment from God, but suffering operated in the sphere of prevention rather than remediation (i.e., for sinful inclinations detected rather than past sins being judged).

Qualification regarding the timing of the execution of the principle. Everyone agreed that divine reaction to righteousness or wickedness was generally not immediate, but how much time lapse could there be without compromising the integrity of the formula? In societies where varying destinies after death are considered possible, true justice may be deferred when not experienced in this life. In the ancient world (Israel included, Egypt excepted) the concept of reward and punishment in the afterlife was not part of the belief system, so the timing issue deepened the mystery rather than providing a resolution. In Christian thinking, however, this is often a basis for theodicy. The qualification is that people sometimes suffer for now, but justice must be viewed over the scope of time. The retribution principle is retained, but its scope is extended into the afterlife.

Qualification regarding the role of justice in the world. This approach suggests that justice is complex and cannot be reduced to a formula like the retribution principle. It recognizes that justice is rarely transparent and requires one to have more information than is readily available. It gives God the benefit of the doubt as it accepts by faith that justice flows from God, who is its fountainhead, regardless of how any given individual is faring. As such it adopts the main statement of the retribution principle (the righteous will prosper and the wicked will suffer) as proverbially and theologically accurate. Yet it denies the corollary that suggests that a person's prosperity or suffering can serve as the basis for discerning whether a person is righteous or wicked. The qualification is that justice is not the sole foundation of how God works in our world because, given a fallen world, perfect justice is not attainable and that the basis for God's operation of the world is his character, not just one attribute or another. God, in his wisdom, is concerned with provisional justice given the parameters of an imperfect world.

WHAT UNDERLIES RETRIBUTION THEOLOGY?

In Israelite theology God is just, and he administers justice in the world. He employs the retribution principle to give insight into his character and to articulate the general parameters of his administration. This activity can be traced on both a corporate and an individual level. The unique shape of the retribution principle within Israelite thought is heavily influenced by two philosophical preconceptions: the existence of only one God and the absence of a belief in reward and punishment in the afterlife.

Corporate level, covenant theme. On a corporate level this theology is evident as it is expressed in the covenant blessings and curses. Consequently, it is also evident in the judgment oracles of the prophets since they pronounce the doom that the Israelites have brought upon themselves by their covenant violations. The corporate aspects of the retribution principle are worked out literarily by the Chronicler (as well as in Samuel-Kings) as he traces its effects through the history of the monarchy. The difference is that while Chronicles puts its emphasis on immediate retribution, Samuel-Kings focuses on delayed retribution. On the corporate level the retribution principle provides for occasional tension (e.g., Ps 44; Esther), but since it can be worked out over the long span of history, it carries less immediacy, urgency or poignancy. Corporate retribution in Israel was a covenant theme, and since covenant violation was rampant, the claim of innocence was difficult to maintain.

Individual wisdom theme. In contrast, the retribution principle on the individual level is a wisdom theme. This connection is laid out plainly in Psalm 1 and is confirmed repeatedly in the central role of the retribution principle in wisdom literature. It is important to note, however, that the biblical text only offers affirmation of the main proposition (the righteous prosper; the wicked suffer), not of the deduced converse corollary (the one who prospers is righteous; the one who suffers is wicked). Logically, the corollary could only be asserted if the main proposition is true universally and consistently and if there are no other reasons for prosperity and suffering. Nevertheless, it appears that the Israelites did tend to extend their expectations to include the corollary, as the book of Job and the need for a book such as Job imply. The tension of the book is created by the corollary as both Job and his friends conclude that his suffering can only be explained as punishment from God. We will return to this below.

Connection to monotheism and afterlife. Since Israel was to believe in only one God who was responsible for every aspect of the cosmos, it was very difficult to absolve him from responsibility for suffering. If he was to be considered just, then they believed that he must maintain the retribution principle. If there was no chance to achieve final justice in the afterlife (more about this in chap. 13), then he was obliged to do so within the lifetime of the individual. Note Psalm 27:13:

> I remain confident of this:
>> I will see the goodness of the Lord
>> in the land of the living.

These factors combined to pose the conundrum of the retribution principle and human experience and led to the principle being used for theodicy. It is in Israel, therefore, that we see the formulation of the inherent connection between the retribution principle and theodicy that becomes commonplace in the history of theological discourse. On the basis of this introduction to the foundation and implications of the retribution principle, we can now turn our attention to the perspectives on the retribution principle found throughout Scripture.

FOR FURTHER REFLECTION

1. What is the retribution principle? Do you ever think like this?

2. How does the book of Job put the retribution principle under the microscope?

3. How does the retribution principle interact with the great symbiosis?

4. How do the retribution principle and theodicy come together?

5. How does the book of Job separate theology from theodicy?

6. What underlies the retribution principle?

TWELVE

THE RETRIBUTION PRINCIPLE
IN WISDOM LITERATURE

In the previous chapter we explored the meaning of the retribution principle and how it was used in the ancient Near East and by the friends of Job to explain the experience of suffering. Now we continue by looking more pointedly at the biblical testimony concerning the principle. We focus on the wisdom literature: Psalms, Proverbs, Ecclesiastes and finally Job itself.

THE RETRIBUTION PRINCIPLE IN PSALMS

The psalmist expects the retribution principle to work (Ps 37; 55:22). He considers himself innocent and therefore expects God to relieve his suffering or trials and thus vindicate him from corollary inferences (Ps 26 and 35). The problem that is most frequently the premise for the psalmist's complaints and his invocation of the retribution principle is the perception that God has abandoned him or is hiding his face from him (e.g., Ps 13; 22:1; 38:21; 44:24). God is not viewed as the cause of his suffering, but God has not come to his aid to relieve his suffering. Yahweh's absence makes one vulnerable to suffering at the hands of the enemies of God and perhaps even to death. What the psalmist longs for is not prosperity but the presence of Yahweh, which brings life and deliverance (Ps 31:14-24; 84; 102:28). In this sense the retribution principle in Psalms could be reformulated more specifically as "the righteous will enjoy God's presence and its accompanying benefits; the wicked will forfeit the presence of God and will suffer the consequences of abandonment."

In contrast to the lament psalms in which the psalmists' circumstances are under discussion, some of the wisdom psalms turn greater attention to the circumstances of others, specifically the wicked. Now instead of trying to understand the suffering of the righteous and the apparent abandonment by God, the psalmists seek to understand the prosperity of the wicked and God's apparent failure to judge those whose actions deserve punishment (e.g., Ps 37 and 49). The retribution principle thus serves as a backdrop to the imprecatory psalms in which the psalmist lists specific things that would have to come upon the wicked in order for the proportionality of the principle to be maintained (cf. Ps 109). If God is administering justice through the retribution principle, then a slap on the wrist will not suffice.

In Psalms, then, we see the expectation that the retribution principle will govern human experience and the repeated affirmation that the principle gives adequate expression to theologically sound expectations. The experiences, however, of inexplicable suffering by the righteous and the observation of apparent prosperity and success of the wicked lead to questions and confusion about God's stance. These testify to their deep-seated misunderstanding of God's commitment to the retribution principle and the resulting misapplication of it.

Psalm 73 is the poem of a wise person who has questioned God because the wicked have prospered and he, a righteous man, has languished. However, when he comes into the presence of God ("I entered the sanctuary of God," Ps 73:17), his perspective radically changes, prompting him to proclaim "surely God is good . . . to those who are pure in heart" (Ps 73:1).

THE RETRIBUTION PRINCIPLE IN PROVERBS

Proverbs actually has some relief to offer in that it clearly positions the retribution principle in the category of proverbial saying, most notably in a variety of permutations in Proverbs 10–12 (see Prov 10:3, 9, 16, 24, 25,

27, 30; 11:5, 6, 18, 19, 21; 12:2, 7, 21). The significance of this cannot be overstated. Proverbial sayings by definition are generalizations, which therefore find their truth in the fact that they stand as probabilities, not as guarantees for what must be true without exception.[1] They are to be interpreted existentially (reflecting a possibility that is observed with some degree of regularity and descriptive of tendencies) rather than universally (reflecting necessity on every occasion). Such statements indicate that there is a higher probability of the stated action than of any of the possible alternatives. To say that Proverbs teaches the type of retribution principle that the three friends and Job represent requires the proverbs to be read as promises or guarantees rather than as showing the best route to a desired conclusion.[2] As Van Leeuwen insightfully argued,[3] it is the "better than" proverbs more than any others that show that proverbs do not make an absolute and mechanical promise that wise behavior will be rewarded and wicked behavior punished. That wisdom, for instance, is better than wealth means not that the two go hand in hand but that the wise person will sometimes have to choose between the two (see Prov 16:16; 28:6).

READING THE RETRIBUTION PRINCIPLE IN ECCLESIASTES

The book of Ecclesiastes contains two different voices. Ecclesiastes 1:12 introduces the autobiographical reflections of Qohelet ("the Teacher/ Preacher") whose voice is heard in Ecclesiastes 1:12–12:7. He famously concludes that life under the sun is meaningless (Eccles 1:9, etc.). One of the reasons why he comes to that viewpoint is because life is unfair. The retribution principle, in other words, doesn't work, and it should.

The most blatant statement of his disappointment comes in Ecclesiastes 7:15:

> In this meaningless life of mine I have seen both of these:
>
>> the righteous perishing in their righteousness,
>>> and the wicked living long in their wickedness.

This is a problem for Qohelet because he has no certain belief in an afterlife (Eccles 3:18-21; 12:1-7). Thus, if there is no justice in this life, then humans have no motivation to live life with wisdom and righteousness. (See in Eccles 7:16-17 his advice to avoid being overly righteous or wise as well as overly wicked or a fool.)

Qohelet's experience (what he sees) of the unfairness of life conflicts with his theology (what he knows) as expressed in a fascinating passage in Ecclesiastes 8:10-15. He begins with what he sees. He sees the wicked honored in life and even after death. Such preferential treatment for the wicked can only lead to the promotion of wicked behavior. All of a sudden, however, he cites his theology: "I know that it will go better with those who fear God, who are reverent before him. Yet because the wicked do not fear God, it will not go well with them, and their days will not lengthen like a shadow" (Eccles 8:12-13). But his theology does not stand up to his experience. In Ecclesiastes 8:14 he asserts that the "righteous . . . get what the wicked deserve, and the wicked . . . get what the righteous deserve." He concludes with what has commonly been regarded as an expression of carpe diem. Since there is no meaning in life, grab whatever enjoyment you can (Eccles 8:15).

While Qohelet's voice occupies the majority of the book, the fact that the second wise man's words frame Qohelet's writings shows that this second man is really the dominant voice, the voice associated with the message of the book. In the epilogue, the second wise man, who is speaking to his son about Qohelet (see Eccles 12:12), appreciates the truth of Qohelet's message. It is true that "under the sun" life is difficult and then you die. It is true that life is unfair. However, the second wise man offers his son what we might call an above-the-sun perspective in the final two verses of the book:

Now all has been heard;
   here is the conclusion of the matter:
Fear God and keep his commandments,
   for this is the duty of all mankind.
For God will bring every deed into judgment,
   including every hidden thing,
      whether it is good or evil. (Eccles 12:13-14)

The second wise man believes that eventually the retribution principle will indeed work but gives no path forward for figuring out a system: our responsibility is to be faithful.

THE RETRIBUTION PRINCIPLE IN JOB

Much has already been covered concerning the retribution principle in the book of Job. In summary, the book offers a modified view of the retribution principle that construes it in proverbial and theological terms—that is, it is useful to describe what God is like and therefore can serve as a basis for identifying general trends in human experience. But the retribution principle offers no guarantees. The book in effect takes a contratheodicy position: rather than defending God's justice, it defends his wisdom. Though it is not a theodicy, it is very interested in the retribution principle and its legitimacy. In the end the retribution principle is rejected as a foundation for divine activity in the human realm, but it is reclaimed on the proverbial and anecdotal level as representative of the character of deity. God delights in bringing prosperity to the righteous, and he takes seriously the responsibility of punishing the wicked. It is therefore of some importance that at the end of the book God restores Job, thus reemphasizing his commitment to the retribution principle properly understood as a theological principle that cannot be employed for either assessment of God's character (theodicy) or of any person's character (which was the view of the human participants in the book). The restoration of Job's prosperity is a reflection on God and his policies. If Job had pursued the restoration of his prosperity, his actions would have reflected his motives and would have meant that the challenger was right. Thus the basic premise of the retribution principle is retained as typically true (righteous prosper, wicked suffer), but since it does not represent a strict formula that is always true, the corollary fails: human beings' wickedness cannot be inferred when they are suffering, nor can their righteousness be inferred when they are prospering.

ISRAELITE THEOLOGY VERSUS BIBLICAL THEOLOGY: THE RETRIBUTION PRINCIPLE

Did the Israelites believe the retribution principle and its converse? A sufficient number of texts demonstrate that they were aware that it was not enforced moment by moment (e.g., Ps 37:7, 25). That is, they realized the possibility of a time lag before the books are balanced on certain occasions. With that caveat they largely accepted the truth of the proposition but were often inclined to treat it as the main determining factor for God's activity. Consequently, they showed a clear inclination to also accept the converse corollary as true and use it to shape their expectations and to formulate their theodicy.

In contrast to this Israelite theology, the biblical theology of the wisdom literature is more cautious and nuanced. The text never affirms the converse corollary (i.e., those who prosper are righteous and those who suffer are wicked), so it cannot be framed as a biblical teaching. Furthermore Proverbs couches the retribution principle in proverbial language, Ecclesiastes casts suspicion on it and the book of Job details its limitations. Thus biblical theology rejects the retribution principle as providing a theodicy, yet embraces it in its theology.

The issue continues to factor in theological discussion into the New Testament. Jesus confronts it explicitly on two occasions. In John 9:1-3, the disciples ask the retribution-principle question, inquiring as to the cause of the malady of the man born blind: "Rabbi, who sinned, this man or his parents, that he was born blind?" Jesus' answer turns them away from the issue of theodicy (indicated by the question of cause) and toward an expanded theology—that suffering should be evaluated not with regard to cause (actions in the past) but with regard to purpose (God's ongoing plan). Thus his reply: "That the works of God might be displayed in him." As in the book of Job, no explanation for the suffering is forthcoming, possible or necessary. Jesus' words stress what is important: to trust God's wisdom and to seek out his purpose.

In Luke 13:1-5 the question is asked concerning whether those who had died in recent tragedies should be considered to have deserved their death. Again Jesus answers in a way that turns the attention away from cause, and even states that a one-to-one correspondence between sin and punishment should not be made. The alternative that he offers is that they should view the incident as a warning. Consistent with John 9, he refuses to engage the question of cause and directs the attention of his audience to purpose.

Paul weighs in on the retribution-principle question in Galatians 6:7: "A man reaps what he sows." Here he states the retribution principle proverbially without neutralizing its theological impact. That he adopts this nuancing is clear in that his teaching regarding suffering does not embrace the converse corollary.

A PRAGMATIC POSTSCRIPT

Based on the above assessment, we must conclude that the retribution principle, properly nuanced and applied, is a biblical teaching about the nature of God and as such is true. We still must be careful to understand it as theology, not theodicy; as proverbial rather than propositional; as operating within the realm of God's wisdom, not just his justice; and as investigated in relation to purpose rather than to cause.

Given this nuancing we can see that a proper understanding of the retribution principle offers yet another argument concerning the bankruptcy of certain popular evangelical movements such as the health-and-wealth, or prosperity, gospel. The Scripture passages used as proof texts for the health-and-wealth gospel are invariably based on an unnuanced reading of the retribution principle that views it as propositional truth that offers promises to be claimed. Simply put, proverbs are not promises and the retribution principle offers no guarantees.

FOR FURTHER REFLECTION

1. What contributions do the various wisdom books make to the question of the retribution principle?

2. How would you summarize the overall attitude of wisdom literature toward the retribution principle?

3. How does this teaching relate to the teaching of the retribution principle in the New Testament?

4. Analyze the modern health-and-wealth, or prosperity, gospel in the light of the teaching of the wisdom literature.

THIRTEEN

DOES JOB BELIEVE IN
THE AFTERLIFE?

As Job and his friends consider all the options to explain or rationalize Job's suffering, one argument is never set forth. No one ever proposes that even though Job is suffering now, he will be rewarded in eternity for his righteousness and perseverance. No one offers an extended understanding of the retribution principle that the scales will be balanced in the rewards and punishments doled out in the afterlife. No one attempts to vindicate the justice of God by taking the long view beyond temporal circumstances. No one offers such solutions because the view of reward and punishment in eternity was not an aspect of the theology of ancient Israel (until perhaps late in the Old Testament time period; Dan 12:1-3) or the ancient Near East.[1] If Job had even known of the possibility of such an option, it would have been easy to propose that he would be vindicated in eternity. Instead, not only does he fail to invoke that alternative, but he consistently and explicitly rules it out.

REFERENCES TO AFTERLIFE IN JOB

The main term used in Hebrew to designate the netherworld is *she'ol*. It is used eight times in the book, seven by Job and one by Zophar. In several of these, *she'ol* is being used generally as a synonym for death or its entryway, the grave.

- Death is final; there is no return (Job 7:9).

- God's ways are deeper than Sheol (Zophar, Job 11:8).

- Job wishes he could be hidden in the netherworld until God's anger passes but knows that this is not possible (Job 14:13).

- Hope dies when the body dies (Job 17:13-16).

- The wicked inexplicably go to Sheol peacefully (Job 21:13).

- Death snatches away those who sin (retribution principle) (Job 24:19).

- God knows all about the realm of the dead (Job 26:6).

  Other discussions that do not use the term *she'ol* include the following:

- Death means being asleep, at rest (Job 3:13; further described in Job 3:17-19).

- Job longs for death, but only for its rest, not for its potential reward or vindication (Job 3:20-22).

- Job has no hope; he will never see happiness once he is gone (Job 7:6-8).

- The realm of death is described as a "place of no return," "the land of gloom and utter darkness" (Job 10:21; cf. Job 16:22).

- Some infer that Job's "hope" expressed in Job 13:15 is a hope for eternity since he speaks of God slaying him. Unfortunately the translation of the verse is problematic. A preferable alternative is "Even though he may slay me, I will not wait [in silence]," or even, "See he will kill me; I have no hope." In this case Job is expressing his intention to give full vent to his complaint.[2]

- Job makes his strongest statement about the finality of death in Job 14:10-14.[3]

- Many interpret Job 19:26-27 as a hope that Job has for the afterlife, but again the translation is very difficult. Rather than Job insisting that he will see God after death, a more likely translation can be seen in this paraphrase, "Despite my peeling skin, I expect to have enough left to come before God in my own flesh [to be restored to favor]."[4]

- A ransom spares the righteous from dying; it does not provide for them after death (Job 33:21-25; see Job 33:28).

- Elihu paints a picture of the exaltation of the righteous enthroned with kings. Modern readers should not be misled by his use of the word "forever" since the Hebrew term refers only to an open-ended situation, ("in perpetuity") rather than to an eternal state (Job 36:7).

We can see, then, that the human characters show no knowledge of reward or punishment after death and do not foresee any explanation that would relieve the tension of the philosophical situation (for Job or for God). When Yahweh arrives to speak, he speaks of this world, not of the mysteries of eternity, so neither does he suggest anything along the lines of resolution in eternity. Furthermore, in the many discussions in the book about the fate of the wicked (e.g., Job 15:20-35; 18:5-21; 20:4-29; 27:13-23; 34:22-30), all of them represent the wicked in this life and finally conclude in their death. The book never extends the punishment of the wicked beyond death.

All of this is consistent with what we know about Israelite beliefs concerning the afterlife. From the information that we have in Scripture, the Israelites showed little distinction from what was believed throughout the regions of Mesopotamia and the Levant. For them, people continued to exist after death, but it was a shadowy, gloomy existence cut off from the world of the living and from God. No hint of reward or punishment is evident in the texts (with the possible exception of Dan 12:1-3).

If the view of the afterlife in Job shows no deviation from that which is found among Israelites, we can turn our attention to the larger context of the Old Testament. Christian beliefs about the afterlife reflect deeply theological issues. Though our relationship with Christ is established by his work in the past and through our lives in the present, it is common to believe that the final form of that relationship is to be achieved only in eternity. For us, our afterlife in heaven is focused on our full sanctification and on receiving the reward of being in God's presence forever. This is the Christian hope, the apotheosis of relationship and the focus of our theology.

For Israel, however, no such hope is evident in the texts, and the afterlife is the least theological aspect of their belief, which focused on life in the covenant. God had not yet provided an instrument to wipe away their sins and provide for their eternal presence with him. Furthermore he had not given any indication by which they understood that it was his intention to do so. For them the afterlife represented an existence where they were cut off from God. In Sheol there was no opportunity to praise God, even though he had access to it (see, for instance, Ps 6:4-5).

A similar situation obtains in the ancient Near East. In the greatsymbiosis way of thinking, people throughout their lives were meeting the needs of the gods so that the gods would provide for them and protect them. The temples and shrines were the center of their focus and the places where rituals were performed. In the netherworld there were no temples and no ways for its denizens to provide for the gods. They had nothing to offer the gods, so the gods did not care about them. Further, they had nothing to fear from the gods because they were already dead. There is nothing theological or spiritual about the afterlife. It is characterized by the absence of such connections. People in the ancient Near East were more interested in retaining their connection with communities of the living (descendants) and the dead (ancestors) than in the connections they might have with the gods.

The literature of the Old Testament provides much less information concerning connection with communities, though ideas like resting with the fathers (Gen 47:30) and remembrance of the dead (Eccles 1:11) are suggestive. Passages, phrases and words that pertain to Israelite beliefs about the afterlife therefore need to be studied for what they tell us and do not tell us. These will in turn further inform us about the backdrop of the book of Job.

WHAT ABOUT SHEOL?

She'ol has no known antecedent or cognate in the ancient world, and its etymology is likewise uncertain.[5] Isaiah 14:9-11 offers the clearest evidence that Sheol is a place where the spirits of the dead dwell, though many times the Old Testament simply uses the term as a synonym for death or the grave (for example, Ps 16:10; Is 28:15). Usage throughout the Old Testament indicates clearly that Sheol is not a desirable place to go, but it is not a place of judgment for sin.

From a survey of the passages that refer to Sheol, the following details can be deduced:

- Those in Sheol are considered separated from God (Ps 6:5; 88:5, 10-12; Is 38:18) though, as previously mentioned, God has access to Sheol.

- Sheol is never referred to as the abode of the wicked alone.

- While Sheol is never identified as the place where all go (though Eccles 6:6 says that "all go to the same place"), the burden of proof rests on those who suggest that there is an alternative.[6]

- Sheol is referred to in human speech as well as in divine speech (Deut 32:22).

- Sheol is a place of negation: no possessions, memory, knowledge or joy.[7]

- It is not a place where judgment or punishment takes place, though it is considered an act of God's judgment to be sent there prematurely. Subsequently, it is inaccurate to translate *she'ol* as "hell" in the Christian sense, for the latter is by definition a place of punishment.[8]

- No reference suggests varying compartments in Sheol. Deepest Sheol (e.g., Deut 32:22) refers only to its location ("below") rather than a lower compartment.

- Logically, one would not expect a distinction between a place of reward and a place of punishment at this juncture since the ultimate criteria for the distinction as we understand it—the work of Christ—was not yet available.

The summary of Robert Martin-Achard captures the salient points:

Sheol is not in fact a place of punishment reserved for the impious, the abode of the perished is not identical with Gehenna; all the departed are in it, and if in their existence in that place there is nothing of comfort, the evil-doer does not suffer eternal punishment there. It will not be until the period when the last of the Old Testament documents are appearing that the Jews, or at least some of them, will modify their ideas about the Beyond: Sheol will sometimes become a temporary abode where the dead are waiting for resurrection and judgment; to ensure the separation of the good and the evil, it will even be divided into several sections, of which one will be a place of bliss for the righteous, and another a place of suffering for the sinful.[9]

HINTS THAT ISRAELITES HOPED FOR SOMETHING BETTER

Despite the information just presented, some scholars contend that there are at least hints in the Old Testament that the Israelites had a hope for something better than Sheol, that they believed they would be in the presence of God. Three phrases are identified in the Psalms that are interpreted as conveying this hope, so we will now examine them more deeply.

Seeing God's face. In Psalm 17:15 the psalmist is confident that he will see the face of God when he awakes. Coupled with this anticipation in at least two places in the Old Testament, the verb "awake" refers to awakening from death (Is 26:19; Dan 12:2). The combination of these two ideas has given interpreters the basis for suggesting that Psalm 17 and other psalms that use the verb "awake" refer to encountering God (seeing his face) after awakening from death. This is to be the experience of those who are upright (Ps 11:7). Psalms 11 and 17 are actually the only two places where the biblical text refers to seeing God's face (using *ḥzh* and *pannim*). Other psalms refer to the psalmist's experience in the temple as seeing God:

- "I have seen [*ḥzh*] you in the sanctuary and beheld your power and your glory" (Ps 63:2).

- Psalm 27:4 expresses the psalmist's desire to dwell in the house of the Lord "all the days of my life, to gaze [*ḥzh*] on the beauty of the LORD and to seek him in his temple."

The question that we must answer, then, is how to determine whether "awaking" is from sleep or from death, and whether "seeing God" is in the sanctuary or in heaven. "Awaking" is attested in both sorts of contexts (cf.

the motif of going to sleep besieged by enemies and awaking with an expectation of God's deliverance, e.g., Ps 3:5; 63:6-7; 139:18) just as "seeing God" is, so we have a methodological conundrum as we try to discern how we would know which meaning was intended by the psalmist.

Returning to Psalm 17 we can see that in the context the psalmist is praying to be delivered from enemies (Ps 17:14) and he seeks vindication (Ps 17:15). Dying would not constitute deliverance and vindication even if he ended up in the presence of God in heaven. This passage makes perfect sense as a reference to waking in the morning and finding the enemy defeated. We should not opt for a metaphorical reading if the text makes perfect sense without reading it that way. Such a passage could not be used to prove that Israelites had a hope for heaven. Ambiguous terms and contexts do not serve well as primary evidence. All these passages can easily be interpreted within the framework of Sheol being the only alternative.

Redeemed from Sheol.

Therefore my heart is glad and my tongue rejoices;
>   my body also will rest secure,
> because you will not abandon me to the realm of the dead,
>   nor will you let your faithful one see decay.
> You make known to me the path of life;
>   you will fill me with joy in your presence,
>   with eternal pleasures at your right hand. (Ps 16:9-11)

The psalmist is confident that God will not abandon him "to Sheol"— that is, that God will not allow him to die ("see decay"). This phrase suggests the idea not that someone is *abandoned* in Sheol but that they are being *consigned* to Sheol by dying.[10] The expressions are ambiguous enough that one might feel justified going either direction. After all, the "path of life" could be either on earth or in heaven, and the words of the psalmist could be construed as indicating that he expects an eternal destiny other than Sheol. In fact the translation "eternal pleasures at your right hand" readily conveys that idea to a modern Christian reader.

Upon investigation we find that nowhere in the Old Testament is the right hand of God a place in the presence of God in heaven. Instead it is at the right hand of God that one finds protection and deliverance from enemies. Such a positioning means either that the person will live rather than die (Ps 118:15-18) or that he will become God's instrument to gain victory over the wicked (Ps 110:1). To what then would "eternal pleasures" refer? The Hebrew word translated "eternal" (*nṣḥ*) is used as an adjective only four other times, always in a temporal context to describe a perpetual condition.[11] The word translated "pleasures" talks of favor and contentment.[12] Here then the sense is that perpetual favor is found in the protection of God's right hand, and therefore the psalmist is content. This is the joy of God's presence in life. Rather than rejecting the psalmist and consigning him to death and the netherworld, the psalmist is confident that God will protect his life by bringing his presence into the psalmist's life and providing perpetual deliverance from his enemies by the power of his right hand.

The New Testament quotation of Psalm 16:10 in Acts 13:35 declares that God has fulfilled this passage by Jesus' resurrection and the preservation of his body. This fulfillment should not be confused with the message of the psalm in its original context.[13] God often reveals to the New Testament authors more meaning than the Old Testament authors knew or could ever have anticipated. It is fully within the purview of the New Testament authors to engage in this expansion of meaning, but the new readings are part of the New Testament authors' authority, not readings to be inserted into the original meaning of the text. Contextual readings in the Old Testament do not lose their significance or authority just because the New Testament expands on them. Therefore Paul's interpretation in Acts, while perfectly acceptable in Acts, cannot be used to prove that the Israelites in the Old Testament period had a concept of being with God in heaven when they died.

Psalm 49:14-15 has also been interpreted as evidence for the Israelites believing there was an alternative destination to Sheol:

They are like sheep and are destined to die;
    death will be their shepherd

(but the upright will prevail over them in the morning).
Their forms will decay in the grave,
far from their princely mansions.
But God will redeem me from the realm of the dead;
he will surely take me to himself.

Here we need to explore what it would mean to the psalmist to be redeemed from the realm of the dead.[14] It is easy for Christian readers to assume that it talks about Jesus redeeming us from hell by his sacrifice on our behalf. But Israelites would not have made any such assumption. The verb translated "redeem" (*pdh*) is used with the object *nephesh* six other times in the Old Testament. In narrative texts the expression is used by David when he asserts that God has delivered him from troubles (2 Sam 4:9; 1 Kings 1:29). In other psalms the wicked will be slain while the righteous will be delivered (Ps 34:22), the psalmist is rescued unharmed from battle (Ps 55:18) and he reflects on his past deliverance (Ps 71:23). All these reflect back on deliverance, and the speaker is clearly still alive, so they do not refer to an after-death experience or hope. The clearest reference is Job 33:28:

God has delivered me from going down to the pit,
and I shall live to enjoy the light of life.

Here Elihu is describing the restoration of the righteous person who is delivered from enemies and negative circumstances. None of these passages use this phrase to indicate a future life in heaven rather than in Sheol. Psalm 30:2-3 uses a different verb but shows clearly that delivering someone from Sheol means preserving them from death:

LORD my God, I called to you for help,
and you healed me.
You, LORD, brought me up from the realm of the dead [= Sheol];
you spared me from going down to the pit.

God "receiving" an individual. In the last line in Psalm 49:15 quoted above, the psalmist is confident that God will "take me to himself." Again, it is easy to anticipate how a Christian reader will interpret this, but we have to begin with a contextual reading. As always an investigation of the words and phrases that are used will lead us to the sense that an Israelite author would have intended and that an Israelite audience would have understood.

First, we should observe that "to himself" is not present in the Hebrew text—it has been added by the translators to try to make a smooth reading. When that happens interpretation cannot help but enter into the equation. Once we know that we are only dealing with the expression "he will take me," we can look at other places where the same is used. Where or how is the psalmist being taken?

Our research shows that Enoch is also taken (Gen 5:24), but likewise that text does not say where he was taken. In Psalm 73:23-24, the text reads,

> Yet I am always with you;
>> you hold me by my right hand.
> You guide me with your counsel,
>> and afterward you will take me into glory.

Here we may think that at last we have an indication of where the psalmist anticipates being taken: "into glory." But again our modern impulses betray us. The word translated here as "glory" (Hebrew *kavod*) never refers to heaven or to God's abode, and the preposition "into" is not used. The word is functioning in this context as an adverb and conveys the idea of being "taken" honorably. Therefore this word indicates not *where* the psalmist is taken but *how* he is taken.

It is now evident that neither Psalm 49 nor Psalm 73 definitively suggests that the individual is being taken somewhere. Our research now leads us to investigate other uses of this verb, especially in other psalms, and so we turn to Psalm 18:16-19:

> He reached down from on high and took hold of me;
>> he drew me out of deep waters.
> He rescued me from my powerful enemy,
>> from my foes, who were too strong for me.
> They confronted me in the day of my disaster,
>> but the Lord was my support.

> He brought me out into a spacious place;
>> he rescued me because he delighted in me.

From this translation it is not easy to spot the verb we are examining, but it occurs at the end of the first line, translated "took hold of me." In this context the sense is clearly a reference to deliverance from enemies and circumstances. When we take the meaning in this clear passage back into the contexts of Psalms 49 and 73, we can see that they also become clear. There is no justification for reading these verses as references to a hope for the afterlife.

In conclusion, then, the three phrases that are often taken as hints that the Israelites had a hope of heaven are used in ways that give no such indication. This conclusion makes sense with many other passages in the Old Testament that suggest they had no such hope. One that could be mentioned is Psalm 27:13:

> I remain confident of this:
>> I will see the goodness of the Lord
>> in the land of the living.

For the Israelite this was an important affirmation because the Israelites did not expect any demonstrations of the goodness of the LORD in the afterlife; Sheol was their only expectation. To counter that we would need a clear, unambiguous passage; we have none until we get to some development in Daniel 12:2.

IMPLICATIONS FOR READING THE BOOK OF JOB

Returning to the book of Job, nothing in the book evidences any deviation from the general Israelite view. Job, like all Israelites, saw God's reward in a long life filled with blessing. Spending eternity with God was not an option to be considered, and there was no balancing of the scales by reward and punishment after death that they were aware of. New ideas began to be introduced and revealed at the end of the Old Testament period and into the intertestamental period. Changes included portraying the dead as individual and conscious, understanding Sheol as having different compartments for the righteous and the wicked,[15] and regarding

Sheol as an intermediate state.[16] But even in the New Testament period, the differences between the Sadducees, who denied the idea of the afterlife, and the Pharisees, who affirmed it, show that Judaism never universally affirmed the idea of the afterlife.

Once we recognize that the Israelites had no hope of heaven and begin to read the contexts of the Old Testament in light of their limited understanding, we gain valuable insight into important theological issues. First, we learn that a relationship with God need not be constructed around a hope of heaven. This is important for Christians to understand because it is too common for people to think that the work of Christ is primarily intended to offer us the benefits of going to heaven and living forever rather than going to hell. Such an understanding is a distortion. The work of Christ makes it possible for us to be in relationship with God now and forever. If we have "signed up" for the benefits, for what we stand to gain, then the question of the challenger can be seen as an indictment against us. He asked, "Does Job serve God for nothing?" We might ask the same about ourselves. Job proved that he *did* serve God for nothing because when all his benefits were taken away, he did not abandon his relationship with God. What if we had none of the benefits (heaven, eternity, etc.)? Would we serve God anyway? We can learn from the book of Job and from Israelite theology that we should focus more on our present relationship with God than on our future benefits. We should be focused on God rather than on ourselves.

Second, when we come to understand the limited revelation that Israel had about the afterlife, we can gain a greater appreciation of the emphasis that was placed on the retribution principle. With no hope of enjoying the benefits of God's justice in eternity, the Israelites believed that if God was indeed just, that justice would have to come into play in this life. Psalm 37 develops this line of thinking in detail. When justice was not evident, as in the case of Job, Israelites were full of questions about what God was doing. Justice was a day-to-day concern.

FOR FURTHER REFLECTION

1. Are you surprised that there is precious little, if any, knowledge of the

afterlife during the Old Testament time period? Why do you think God waited until later in history to disclose teaching about the afterlife?

2. Imagine yourself living during the Old Testament period. Would not knowing about the afterlife affect your passion for God? Why or why not?

3. How does realizing that Job did not have a belief in the afterlife change your understanding of his character?

FOURTEEN

LEARNING ABOUT THE COSMOS
FROM THE BOOK OF JOB

The book of Job contains more extensive discussion of the cosmos and God's role in it than any other book in the Bible with the possible exception of Psalms. The major sections are Job 9:5-9 (Job), 26:7-14 (Job), 28:20-28 (narrator), 36:27-38 (Elihu), 37:3-13 (Elihu) and 38–39 (Yahweh).

JOB'S VIEW OF THE COSMOS

We have already noted that much of the theology propounded by the human characters in the book of Job is wrong-headed at some level—distorted, misguided or founded on false premises. We might therefore inquire whether the speeches in the book of Job are also offering a flawed view of the cosmos and its operations. Such a question can be answered from either the perspective of the ancient reader or the perspective of the modern reader. From the ancient reader's perspective the discussions of cosmic geography and the operations of the cosmos do not differ from opinions affirmed in the rest of the Bible. Furthermore, what we find in Job is basically in line with the thinking of the time throughout the ancient Near East, except with regard to the identity of the controlling deity. That is to say, the basic beliefs about the shape of the cosmos and the level of divine involvement in the cosmos were fairly consistent throughout the ancient world. The main point of distinction, which we will explore in some detail, concerns whether the cosmos operates on the foundation of justice. This question was more central to an Israelite theology and is of particular concern in Job.

From our perspective as modern readers, we would find the view of the cosmos in the ancient world (and Job) quaint and antiquated. Having no means available to explore the workings of the cosmos, the ancients were left to rely on their observations. The discussions of the shape of the cosmos and its internal operations that we find in Job are often couched in poetry, but that does not mean that they are constructed of poetic metaphors that do not accurately express what they thought about the cosmos (like we would speak of the setting sun). Certainly the book uses metaphors occasionally in the passages about the cosmos, but we cannot maintain that those metaphors conceal a view of the cosmos that was actually much like ours. As modern readers we would conclude that what the book of Job understands as the shape and internal operation of the cosmos is wrong, but no corrective is going to be offered in the book. The Bible is not concerned with providing an authoritative cosmic geography; rather it works within its own cognitive environment.

God did not need to give ancient readers a more advanced understanding of science in order to reveal himself. We all recognize that scientific understanding changes constantly. If God's revelation were embedded in a particular scientific view, there would be no room for further investigation. Statements about the operation of the world cannot easily be so general as to fit the current knowledge and understanding of any generation. Revelation connected to the science of one period would constitute anachronism for earlier periods and would quickly become obsolete as new ideas become old. After all, science is not simply a compilation of facts; it expresses society's consensual understanding of how the world works.[1]

When we read the book of Job, then, we should not approach it as if God has concealed modern scientific truth in ancient guise. In what has come to be known as a concordist hermeneutic, some modern interpreters, concerned about the authority of the Bible or about the conver-

gence between the Bible and our understanding of the natural world, have
attempted to find in the biblical text expression of scientific principles
unknown to the writers of the time. For example, they read Job 36:27-28
as if it alluded to the water cycle of evaporation, condensation and pre-
cipitation. The problem with this approach is that it reads the inspired
words of Scripture to mean more than they meant to the ancient audience.
That would be no surprise, say the concordists, since God is the true
author of Scripture and we see the same thing happening in prophecy and
fulfillment. We do indeed see this phenomenon in prophecy and fulfillment, but the analogy does not hold. When the New Testament authors
offer a fulfillment, they are extending the significance of the prophecy text
as inspired writers who have insight into meaning that God intended. If
we try to do the same thing in our concordism, we are presuming to have
insight into God's meaning and intentions on our own authority. We
should be hesitant to do that.

We might easily claim that even though the ancient readers of Job
36:27-28 would not have inferred a modern understanding of the water
cycle from it, it nevertheless conveys truth about the water cycle and we
therefore find convergence of truth between God's Word and God's world.
Be that as it may, we could not and should not adopt an apologetics stance
to prove the Bible true because it divinely anticipated modern science.
This approach can undermine biblical authority because it vests the imagination of the modern reader with the right to provide new meanings.

An alternative approach to these passages is through an understanding
that God's revelation has made accommodation for the ancient Israelite
audience. Effective communication requires a common ground of famil-
iarity between communicator and audience. If God had spoken of tectonic
plates, planets in orbit or supernovae, the target audience would have
simply been confused. Certainly God could have patiently explained
those concepts, but that was not the task that he undertook. He was revealing himself, not the details of cosmic geography.

This accommodationist view has sometimes been considered problematic because it seems to imply that the Bible contains errors. The sky
is not a solid canopy holding up waters above the earth. The sun, moon

and stars are not inside this solid water barrier. The earth is not a flat disk. When we embrace biblical authority or even inerrancy, however, we are adopting a view that pertains to those things that the Bible *affirms* or, to put it another way, those things the Bible *intends to teach*. That is, we are attaching authority to that which is the focus of the revelation. For the sake of clear communication, God uses incidentals that are believed by his target audience in order to reveal the truths that he wants to convey. Scriptural authority resides in God's revelatory message, not in the incidentals he uses to communicate that message. Inerrancy describes the nature of revelation and our confidence that it is true. God is who he says he is. He has done what he says he has done. His motives and purposes are what the Bible proclaims them to be.

More important then is the question of how God works in the cosmos because that *is* the question that hangs in the balance in the book. In the ancient world as a whole, in Israel specifically and in the book of Job in particular, God was intimately involved in running the cosmos. Yet even as we affirm that, we recognize that people of the ancient world thought very differently from the way we think about the operations of the natural world.

Most importantly, in the ancient world they had no clearly developed concept of that which was "natural." We speak of natural science, the natural world and natural laws, and most of our discussions about science and the Bible focus on trying to determine what was natural and what was supernatural. Can the ten plagues be explained in natural terms? Can we offer a natural explanation of the sun standing still? Did water come out of the rock when Moses struck it because there was an aquifer flowing just beneath the surface? Did the Assyrian army die of the plague?

All our terminology is embedded in these ideas. For example, one cannot speak of intervention or even miracles without a worldview that distinguishes between what is natural and what is supernatural because intervention assumes God's supernatural actions reaching into the world of natural occurrences, and calling something a miracle asserts that no natural explanation can suffice.

People did not think in these categories in the ancient world. On the large scale of cosmic operations, they believed God (using the singular, though in the rest of the ancient world, the plural would be more appropriate) was behind everything that happened. There were no "natural" events. Furthermore if God was behind all of these events, they concluded that the events themselves must represent the will of God. Given a belief that God was just, they would therefore look for his hand of justice in the events. Alternatively one could conclude that God was disengaged or capricious, or that there were other forces in the world to be reckoned with.

Modern Christians believe that God is indeed active in the operations of the cosmos and the events that occur. Today, however, the questions become much more complex because of our acceptance of "natural" cause and effect. What is the book of Job revealing (not just passively believing) about God's involvement in the cosmos? Should we feel compelled to view it in the same way they did? The likely answer is both yes and no. We should certainly believe that God is intimately involved in the operations of the universe. Nevertheless we need not jettison our category of natural cause and effect understood properly. Nor should we believe that God's involvement in the cosmos requires that the cosmos reflect his attributes.

COSMIC GEOGRAPHY

The cosmic geography reflected in the book of Job includes

- "Pillars of the heavens" (Job 26:11). People of the ancient world believed that the sky was solid, though there were various opinions in the ancient world about what it was made of. However this barrier was constructed, it was logical to believe that something held up the sky.

- Pillars of the earth (Job 9:6). The ancients believed that something solid must hold up the flat disk of the earth, but of course then they needed to explain what those pillars rested on.

- "He suspends the earth over nothing" (Job 26:7). The translation of this verse and therefore the ideas that it communicates are a matter of some controversy. The first line of the verse pertains to the mythological conception of the heavenly sphere where the gods meet in council. It associates them with that which is at the perimeter of the ordered realm, likely the "waters above" (NIV "empty space").[2] The second line contrasts with a statement that either the earth or the netherworld (the term here could mean either) is hung on (not over) "nothing." This last word, which only occurs here in the Bible, is the most difficult in a verse full of difficult words. We would tentatively suggest that it be understood as referring to the non-ordered realm on which the earth rests, an indirect reference to the waters below.[3]

- The horizon line was considered the "boundary between light and darkness" (Job 26:10).

- "Ends of the earth" (Job 28:24; 37:3; "edges" in Job 38:13) reveals the understanding that the earth was flat and therefore had "ends."

- Chamber of the tempest (Job 37:9). The idea that wind, rain, hail, and so on were kept in storehouses in the heavens was a common view (cf. Job 38:22, 24).

- Stars and their paths inscribed or decreed (Job 38:31-33). Some in the ancient world believed the stars and the paths that they followed were inscribed on the underside of the solid dome of the sky. The word translated "laws" here refers to that which is inscribed and therefore decreed, and may imply this cosmological idea (cf. perhaps Ps 8:3).

The impact of all of this is minimal. These texts testify to the perspective that was common in the ancient world, so it is no surprise to see these ideas built into the book. Certainly Scripture is not mandating that we all think this way, but neither is its authority jeopardized by the presence of these perceptions of the cosmos. Instead the book is vested in talking about God's ordering of the cosmos and his control over it.

GOD'S ORDERING OF THE COSMOS

In the ancient world of which Israel was a part, creation was most importantly an act of ordering the cosmos—making everything function the way God wanted it to. It was not sufficient just to make objects; everything was to be brought under his control, and every object must serve its purpose. When that was accomplished, it was good: functioning the way that God designed it to function.

God's seven-day process in Genesis 1 started with non-order. Non-order refers to a primordial situation in which the raw materials were present but still needed to be assigned their roles and functions according to God's purposes. Non-order is not evil; it is just not yet completed in its final form—a work in progress. His initial work of ordering creation did not result in total order by design. The sea is a place of non-order, and there was an outside the garden that presumably did not feature the same level of order as inside the garden. People were created to work alongside God to continue the process as vice-regents in his image. It is not that God was somehow incapable of achieving total order from the beginning. In his wisdom he chose to work through an extended process and bring people into partnership along the way.[4] In this way, even before the fall, people lived in a world that was characterized by both established order and continuing non-order.

Then the situation got worse. When Adam and Eve took the fruit from the tree of wisdom (i.e., "knowledge of good and evil," Gen 2:17), it was their intention to "be like God" (Gen 3:4). Order is the fruit of wisdom. God is the source and center of both. Therefore one of the ways to "be like God," particularly with regard to wisdom, is to try to make oneself the source and center of order. Rather than bringing increased order (as people were supposed to be doing alongside God), people set themselves up as an alternative source and center of order and wisdom in their attempt to usurp that role from God, and the result was disorder. Since that time we have lived in a world that is characterized by order and continuing non-order, and dominated by disorder, as we each see ourselves as the center and each go astray, each toward his or her own way.

This perspective on the way that the Israelites thought about the world around them is very important for understanding the teaching of the book of Job. In a strict application of the retribution principle, the automatic conclusion would be that Job was suffering the consequences of disorder—not just general disorder but his own individual disorder: he had presumably sinned in sufficient proportion to warrant the disasters that overtook him. Such a conclusion could only be reached if disorder were the only possible explanation for suffering. An additional possible explanation for suffering is continued non-order in the world.

This insight makes the important point that the world around us is not fully endowed with God's attributes. The fact that justice flows from the nature of God does not mean that everything that happens in the world is just. Likewise God's goodness is not always reflected in the world, nor does he exert his sovereignty throughout. None of this suggests that his justice, goodness or sovereignty is flawed or incomplete. In his wisdom God has decided to bring order gradually. He can impose his will at any time and in any way, but he has set up a realm where non-order remains and where disorder is allowed to intrude. Therefore the operations of the world, while making his presence known to people so they are "without excuse" (Rom 1:20), do not reflect the nature, character or attributes of God.

This perspective is nowhere clearer in the book than in Yahweh's own insistence that rains and floods are not to be automatically considered responses of his justice (i.e., for blessing or punishment) since it rains "where no one lives" (Job 38:25-27). Many of the phenomena that we term "natural disasters" on the cosmic level (e.g., hurricanes, tsunamis, earthquakes, tornadoes, droughts and famines, plagues and epidemics), all the way down to devastating experiences at the biological level (e.g., mutations), can be identified as aspects of non-order in the world. They can have a severely negative impact, and God could potentially use them as punishment, but they are not intrinsically evil in any moral sense. They are not impervious to God's control, but neither can they be considered instruments wielded in judgment. They are not independent of him, but we should not picture him with a remote-control device. These forces are subject to his bidding just as humans are, though we are not robots.

In conclusion we cannot derive detailed knowledge of God's nature from the experiences that we or others have. The continued existence of non-order and disorder means that God has not imposed his attributes on the world; therefore the operations of the world are not just and the retribution principle cannot offer a basis for determining the cause of our experiences with any level of confidence. God can use disasters or disease in acts of judgment, but we would never know whether he is doing so unless we had a prophetic voice to convey a message to that effect. Those who lose their lives in a hurricane are no more wicked than those who are spared, but through these events we should all be warned (Lk 13:1-5).

How then is the world under his control? How can God tolerate a world that does not consistently bend to his nature? Rather than following our natural inclination to evaluate these evidences as a sign of God's weakness, negligence or capriciousness, we should see this approach as a result of his grace. If the cosmos were to be brought into total conformity to justice, there would be no room for sinners—forgiven or otherwise. Instead love constrains him, and we are recipients of his mercy in unknown and uncounted ways. All such decisions concerning justice, mercy, compassion or punishment come under the governance of his wisdom. When we affirm his wisdom we assert that none of us could do a better job of running the world. Job thought he could, and God called his bluff (Job 40:10-14).

GOD'S CONTROL OF THE COSMOS

How then should we think about God's control of the cosmos? In our discussion of cosmic geography we saw that the book made few explicit references to aspects of the cosmic geography of the ancient world even though inferences could be made from indirect statements. In contrast we can see that the book has a lot more to say about God's involvement in the control of the cosmos:

- "Shakes the earth" (Job 9:6)
- Darkens the sun (Job 9:7)
- "Seals off the light of the stars" (Job 9:7)
- "Stretches out the heavens" (Job 9:8); "spreads out the . . . skies" (Job 26:7)
- Makes the constellations (Job 9:9)
- "Suspends the earth" (Job 26:7)

- "Wraps up the waters in . . . clouds" (Job 26:8)
- "Covers the face of the . . . moon" (Job 26:9)
- "Marks out the horizon on the face of the waters" (Job 26:10)
- Sets a "boundary between light and darkness" (Job 26:10)
- "Churned up the sea" (Job 26:12)
- "Established the force of the wind" (Job 28:25; cf. 37:9)
- Decreed the path for rain and thunderstorms (Job 28:26)
- Draws out water to make rain (Job 36:27-28; 37:6, 11)
- "Spreads out the clouds" (Job 36:29)
- Brings lightning and thunder (Job 36:29-30, 32-33; 37:2-5, 11)
- Provides snow and ice (Job 37:6, 10)
- "Laid the earth's foundation" (Job 38:4)
- Established dimensions of the earth (Job 38:5-6)
- Closed "the sea behind doors" (Job 38:8-11)
- Sends hail (Job 38:22-23)
- Gave the wild donkey its habitat (Job 39:5)

Many more could be added if we extrapolated from the rhetorical questions that God asks Job in Job 38. When he asks Job if he can do this or that, in many cases the implication is that God can or does do those things.

In the above list about half of the items refer to what God did in creation. God's creating was one way that God imposed his control on the cosmos. To the extent that the order he imposed remains, he continues to control the cosmos in those ways. In the ancient world there is not as clean a distinction between creating and sustaining—especially when ongoing functions are under discussion.

The other half of the list enumerates cosmic events for which we could easily ascribe natural causes (again recalling that identifying natural cause and effect does not remove God from the picture). In our way of thinking that would mean that God's control of the cosmos is expressed in the way that he designed it and in the consistent operation of what we call "natural laws." This would mean that whatever circumstances for good or ill come into our lives according to the way the cosmos operates is under God's jurisdiction, but these events result from the way God set up the cosmos in the past rather than in decisions he makes day by day.

We don't raise questions about the effect of gravity in a certain situation; neither should we ask why it rained in one place and not in another. We don't raise questions about why a bone breaks when we fall; neither should we ask why one person gets diabetes or cancer and another does not. God's wisdom is founded in the world that he chose to create, not in each expression of gravity or cell division. God created our nervous systems as a means of protecting our bodies, but with that system comes the inevitability of pain. When a diabetic loses the sensitivity of the nerve endings in his or her extremities, life and health can be threatened. We must understand that God's control is more connected to the cosmic system than to our individual, personal experiences or conduct.

Why did God devise the system the way that he did? This is not a question that we can answer, but we can say that he did not do it for the sake of justice. Justice is not the linchpin of the cosmos. The forces that God built into the world are not discerning, volitional or moral, and God does not micromanage. There is more to the world than justice, and we should be glad of it, because if justice were at the core of everything, we would not exist. In his wisdom God orders the cosmos to work the way that it does. He is able to interfere or even micromanage, but that is not typical. In its fallen state the world can only operate by his wisdom, not by his justice.

FOR FURTHER REFLECTION

1. Analyze the following statement from the chapter: "The Bible is not concerned with providing an authoritative cosmic geography; rather it works within its own cognitive environment."

2. What is the problem with using the book of Job to produce a scientific understanding of the cosmos?

3. Contrast the concordist and accommodationist views of the relationship between science and the book of Job.

4. What did the cosmos look like to Job?

5. Why did God devise the system that he did?

FIFTEEN

THE THEOLOGY OF SUFFERING IN THE BOOK OF JOB

We are using the term *suffering* to cover a wide range of phenomena. It can be physical: from minor but chronic pain to significant debilitating pain, from conditions like migraines to the results of an injury, such as the phantom pain of an amputee. It can also be psychological: from separation from a loved one to the deep grief of loss, from the shame of guilt to the anxiety connected to fears, from living in an abusive relationship to coping with broken family relationships. It can be circumstantial: living with an eating disorder, HIV or a neurological disease. It can be surrogate: trying to care for the aged or the terminally ill, suffering because those who are near us suffer. Finally, it can be systemic: from those whose lives are threatened by repressive regimes and those who have become victims of human trafficking to those who live under circumstances in which hunger and disease are taking lives daily. Suffering can break us, and it is characteristic of the broken world in which we live.

Given this broad definition of *suffering*, what then is meant by a theology of suffering? The term *theology* refers to how we think about God. Therefore a theology of suffering explores how we think about God in connection to suffering. Such a theology would include the larger questions: Why has God created a world in which such suffering can exist, and why does he allow it to continue? But it can also include the deeply personal questions: Why is this happening to me? Is God trying to teach me something? Did I do something wrong?

For some people, approaching a theology of suffering leads them to formulate a theodicy. A theodicy attempts to provide a consistent, holistic explanation of why the world works the way that it does and, in the process, to vindicate God with regard to his role in it. In a theodicy the main intent is to explain how a God who is all good, all-powerful and characterized by justice and compassion can allow (let alone create) a world in which suffering is so pervasive. A skeptic would view such an undertaking as an effort to make excuses for an inadequate God. Such skeptics regularly conclude, given the amount of suffering in the world, that there either is no God or that a God who would allow this is not worthy of worship. This is the result of a failed theodicy.

Others construct a frail theodicy such as that maintained by Job and his friends. This sort of theodicy may help some people explain their present set of circumstances, but when their circumstances change, or when they try to apply this theodicy to a wider range of experiences, it is found wanting.

Many theologians would claim that it is presumptuous of humans to think that they can devise a theodicy. Most importantly the premise behind this thinking is that God is in no need of our help to defend his decisions. He is above vindication because he is beyond our ability to explain. Attempts to vindicate God would have to work under the assumption that he has to conform to some outside criterion (which he does not) and that we could sit at the judge's bench to determine whether he succeeded in meeting our expectations. This is eventually the position at which the book of Job arrives when Job submits to God in silence (Job 42:1-6).

As we consider the theology of suffering in the book of Job, then, we approach the task with humility (God is not to be called to account) and with a sense of reality (a full recognition of the extent of suffering in the world and in our lives). We neither ask God to account for himself nor ask why our lives and the world are the way they are. We ultimately want to know what the book of Job can help us learn about how to think about God in the light of suffering, whether personal or universal. We will turn our attention to that question when we get to the chapter on the message of the book of Job (chap. 18). In the remainder of this chapter we will consider six perspectives on suffering that will lay the foundation for the eventual conclusions of the book of Job.

SUFFERING IS THE LOT OF ALL HUMANITY

We all know that none of us is immune to suffering because all have experienced it at one level or another. When we are going through times that are relatively free of suffering, however, we must not insulate ourselves from the suffering of others around us and throughout the world. Suffering should arouse our compassion and motivate us to action. Therefore a theology of suffering is less interested in helping us cope and more interested in leading us to care. When we experience it ourselves we can be more sympathetic to the plight of others. We should be constantly preparing ourselves for times of suffering. Such a frame of mind is not fatalism but realism. No matter how severe our suffering might be, there are always those who are suffering more. This realization may help us to put our suffering to good use as our minds are opened to the plight of others.

A CONTINGENCY OF THE CREATION IN PROCESS

As we discussed in the previous chapter, the biblical view of the world is one in which order has not yet been fully achieved. While we cannot imagine what a fully ordered world would be like, we can recognize that both non-order and disorder are responsible for suffering at one level or another. God's design was to create us with nervous systems that warn us of potential harm through what we perceive as pain. Furthermore God created us with emotions through which we can experience hurt feelings. If we are capable of love, we are vulnerable to pain. Therefore in this life and in this world, with these sorts of bodies, suffering is unavoidable. We have to build this into our expectations. "Normal" cannot be defined as a life free of suffering, or even a brief time free of suffering. We might consider such times to be ideal, but even when we do not individually experience suffering, we cannot shut out the suffering that exists worldwide. Normal has to be redefined given the realities of creation in process. If we expect suffering, it will not seem anomalous when we experience it. This perspective does not make suffering easier to bear, but it can affect our attitude about it. We have not been singled out.

NOT INTRINSICALLY CONNECTED TO SIN

Even in the broader perspective on a universal scale, suffering that we experience is not fully explained by sin. Using the terms that we established in chapter fourteen, suffering can often be the result of disorder (sin), but it can also be experienced as the result of non-order (creation incomplete). Consequently we would have to conclude that personal suffering is likewise not intrinsically connected to sin and certainly not always connected to our own personal sin.

Two caveats must immediately be noted. First, examples can easily be cited in which someone's suffering is indeed the direct natural consequence of sin that person has committed. Those who have abused alcohol or drugs should not be surprised that they are suffering the physical effects of such abuse. Second, unquestionably God can use suffering as punishment for sin. Nevertheless we should never presume that our suffering is an act of punishment by God. We can well believe that we will reap what we sow (Gal 6:7), but that does not allow us to draw a one-to-one correspondence between behavior and circumstances. Suffering can, however, lead us to evaluate our lives to determine whether we are on the right path.

We can therefore conclude that the retribution principle is inadequate. As we noted earlier the retribution principle serves as an instructive part of theology but cannot provide a theodicy (chap. 5). We all sow things that, mercifully, we do not reap, and we all reap some things that we did not sow. The most important lesson to draw from this is that we should never assume that someone who is suffering has done something to deserve pain or punishment. This sort of thinking represents the most dangerous result of mistaken theology and is severely criticized by the book of Job.

INTO THE ARMS OF GOD'S LOVE

A friend shared with me a paragraph from Arthur J. Gossip's sermon "But When Life Tumbles In, What Then?" This pastor had recently lost his wife and explained in these words to his congregation why this devastating loss had not resulted in a crisis of faith. His words offer us an important perspective about why suffering should lead us to cling to God rather than to reject him.

> I do not understand this life of ours. But still less can I comprehend how people in trouble and loss and bereavement can fling away peevishly from the Christian faith. In God's name, fling to what? Have we not lost enough without losing that too? If Christ is right— if, as He says, there are somehow, hidden away from our eyes as yet, still there, wisdom and planning and kindness and love in these dark dispensations—then we can see them through. But if Christ was wrong, and all that is not so; if God set His foot on my home crudely, heedlessly, blunderingly, blindly, as I unawares might tread upon some insect in my path, have I not the right to be angry and sore? If Christ was right, and immortality and dear hopes of which He speaks do really lie a little way ahead, we can manage to make our way to them. But if it is not so, if it is all over, if there is nothing more, how dark the darkness grows! You people in the sunshine may believe the faith, but we in the shadow must believe it. We have nothing else.[1]

Trusting in God's wisdom is the strongest counsel the Bible has to offer; it must suffice. One of the ways we trust God's wisdom is by refraining from inquiring why God *did* such a thing to us, or even why he *allowed* it to happen. God is never uninvolved in cause, but neither should we assume that he is directly involved in causation.[2] Likewise examining what he permitted or did not prevent takes us into territory in which no navigational tools exist to give us bearings. None of the language, degrees or concepts of causation is adequate to inform us regarding God's involvement. God is neither micromanaging every circumstance nor signing off on them. Yet it would be a mistake in the opposite direction to think that he was distant and disengaged. On this topic John Polkinghorne suggests that terminology like "allow" should not be used in a way that implies blame. "The suffering and evil of the world are not due to weakness, oversight, or callousness on God's part, but, rather, they are the inescapable cost of a creation allowed to be other than God."[3] Our overly simplistic reactions need to be replaced with an impulse to trust our Creator.

AN OPPORTUNITY TO DEEPEN OUR FAITH

Whatever suffering we have experienced in life has made us who we are (Rom 5:3). Sometimes suffering causes a person to become incredibly strong in faith; other times the sufferer is left broken and empty. It does not suffice to find strength only in some sort of silver lining because too often no bright side emerges. We cannot expect that anything will come along to make it all better. Some things we cannot recover from. Our faith will be deepened through suffering if we commit to honoring God and living for him in whatever circumstances he places us. This sort of thinking does not help us salvage the retribution principle because it does not offer a reason for suffering—only a response to it.

We cannot conclude on the basis of biblical teaching that God wants everyone to be healthy and happy so we only need to ask in faith for our situation to be resolved. We can pray for healing for ourselves and for others, and we should have faith that God can heal us if he so chooses. But we are not in a position to make demands of him. Perhaps a more important prayer is a plea for God to strengthen us to endure the suffering and to be faithful to him throughout the time of trial and crisis. It is important that we not respond with disappointment in God. God does not fall short or suffer lapses in execution of his purposes. If it seems to us that he has not met our expectations, we should reexamine our expectations. We should seek to honor God when life is at its lowest. We should strive to trust him even when hope is gone.

PARTICIPATING IN CHRIST'S SUFFERING

In the Sermon on the Mount, Jesus spoke of the blessing of suffering and being persecuted for the sake of the gospel and the kingdom (Mt 5:10-12;

cf. 1 Pet 2:19-25; 3:14; 4:12-19). This jarring statement runs contrary to what we have come to identify as the retribution principle. Since the times of the psalmists (and likely before that), faithful people of God expected him to bring defeat to their enemies. Christ proclaimed a different way, which would bring triumph through defeat, to which the cross compellingly testifies. We should not always expect deliverance from enemies (Phil 3:10).

Be that as it may, suffering from illness is not the same as suffering at the hands of enemies. We can count it all joy when we suffer for Christ, but when enemies are not involved and a stand for the kingdom is not in the equation, can our suffering still be viewed as participation in Christ's suffering? At least in some ways it can. The suffering of Christ on the cross was not only suffering for what is right, but it was also physical suffering. Perhaps we could say that in this way he suffered with us: as a human he participated in our suffering, and he endured it (Phil 2:7-8). Besides the excruciating physical pain he suffered, he experienced the anguish of betrayal and the pain of rejection (as he fulfilled Is 53:3-4; see Mt 8:17). We have no record of him contracting serious diseases or suffering pain from injury, but we are assured that he takes all our diseases and injuries upon himself and suffers what we suffer.

FOR FURTHER REFLECTION

1. Is it always, or even usually, possible for us to identify the reason why we are suffering?

2. How does the book of Job help us when we suffer?

3. What are the factors that keep us from seeing our suffering as a participation in Christ's suffering?

SIXTEEN

JOB'S VIEW OF GOD

In this chapter we will address the view of God held by the character Job rather than the view of God the author of the book would like the reader to adopt. They are different. The book is not demonstrating that Job is thinking rightly about God. The rhetorical strategy of the book is not dependent on Job's theology being irreproachable; neither is he intended to be a model for our own theology. Job is remarkable for his persistence and for maintaining his integrity (see chap. 7). Job's reactions to God are similar to some of those we might also have voiced given a similar position. His initial response is acceptance (Job 1:21; 2:10), but that does not last. As the book unfolds he accuses God of being petty and unjust and seeks to manipulate him. These are not attitudes or behaviors we should adopt. Instead we need to allow Job his human weakness: a deficient view of God. After all, if his view of God was impeccable, why would God address him out of a whirlwind at the end of the book (Job 38:1)?

JOB'S VIEW OF GOD AS PETTY

In chapter seven we have already given some attention to Job's ritual conscientiousness on behalf of his children in Job 1:4-5. We suggested that one plausible reading of this vignette did not show Job in a positive light. Instead it served as a bridge to the scene in heaven, paving the way for the challenger to question whether Job served God for nothing. Conscientious attention to ritual is admirable, but in the vignette it is excessive in that it seeks to redress (1) others' standing (2) without their initiation (3) for something they have no reason to think that they did and (4) for a supposed potential offense that would have been utterly private ("in their hearts"). The challenger would have every reason to observe this behavior and conclude that Job is overcompensating in ritual due to an unhealthy belief that God is petty. Job is suspect not only because he seems over-attentive to God's rewards but also because he seems over-attentive to God's judgment. We should be clear that this does not mean that Job sinned in his over-attentiveness to God, but it does open up the question of his motives.

Job's opinion of God as overly vigilant and petty unfolds throughout the book and can be seen explicitly in Job 7:17-21 and 14:3-6. Since Job knows that he has not done anything to warrant the magnitude of suffering that he has experienced, and continues to maintain the retribution principle, he can only conclude either that God is unjust or that his standards are too exacting. All humans are frail, and, in Job's opinion, God has not taken that sufficiently under advisement (Job 10:4-8).

This reaction of Job's is fairly typical even today. It is not unusual for someone who is suffering to say things like, "What does he *want* from me? I have done everything he has asked!" People begin evaluating their lives and start to wonder whether God is responding to some small slight or lapse a decade ago. God is perfect and wants us to "be perfect as [he] is perfect" (Mt 5:48),[1] but that does not mean that he mercilessly calls us to account for minute deviations. Small offenses are offenses nonetheless, but Scripture assures us that God knows our weaknesses and realizes that we are frail (Ps 103:8-18).

JOB'S VIEW OF GOD AS UNJUST

Job's suspicion that God was petty had emerged even in the prologue and was alluded to perhaps as early as his lament (Job 3:25?). It is clearly affirmed in his first speech (Job 7:17-21). In contrast, Job's assertions that God's actions cannot be gainsaid are at the heart of his early affirmations (Job 1:21; 2:10). As the book proceeds, however, Job becomes less reticent as he moves from calling God to account for his exacting standards to eventually calling him to account for the justice of his ways. The erosion begins when Job expresses his desire to face his supposed accuser (God) in court. He wants to know what the charges are against him—demanding what we might call a writ of habeas corpus. If that were as far as it went, we could not find reason to criticize. However, Job proceeds to accuse God of abuse of power. It is a subtle transition from "if it is a matter of justice, who can challenge him?" (Job 9:19) to "he destroys both the blameless and the wicked" (Job 9:22). The judge of all the earth should do what is right by not "treating the righteous and the wicked alike" (Gen 18:25). Since Job believes that God does not discriminate between the righteous and the wicked, he asserts that God does not do what is right (*mishpat*, the word for justice). God's rebuke of Job in Job 40:8 makes it clear that Job has considered God to be unjust. Job claims in Job 19:7 that there is no *mishpat* and in Job 27:2 that God has withheld *mishpat* from him (cf. Job 34:5).

By the time we get to Job's second series of speeches, we find the strongest negative statements about God that Job makes in the dialogue section of the book. In Job 16:9-14 he lines up his accusations against God as an assailant, an opponent, a betrayer and a warrior with no pity. Once we move to the discourse section, Job has become outspoken in his outrage against the God he now accuses of reckless cruelty (the thrust of the Hebrew word, *'akhzar,* in Job 30:21).

This inclination to escalate the rhetoric that we observe in Job's castigation of God is likewise frequently characteristic of our modern reactions. If we expect justice in every circumstance we face in life, we are going to be disappointed, and in our frustration that disappointment can take God as its focus. Someone has to be blamed! As we have seen (chap. 11), we (like Job) have come to accept the premise that if justice flows from God and he is all-powerful, then we should expect our experience to reflect the justice of God. This flawed thinking assumes that the cosmos is stamped with the attributes of God—a view that we discarded (chap. 14). It mistakenly concludes that it is in keeping with God's plan day by day to ensure that justice is done on the earth. When justice is not seen to be fulfilled in our world and in our lives, it is easy to conclude that God is making decisions but that justice is not driving those decisions. If he is exercising power unguided by justice, then he becomes like the chaos creature Job portrays him to be. As such he is not bringing order, nor is he the source of order; he represents non-order.

In this world that features order, non-order and disorder, justice cannot reign. That is by God's design and, we assert, a reflection of his wisdom. He is the source and center of order, but neither non-order nor disorder is outside of his control. For example, he uses both at times for bringing judgment: the flood (using non-order) and the destruction of the temple and Jerusalem by Nebuchadnezzar (using disorder). In these cases the indictable offenses are established by the text. Prophets such as Jeremiah and Habakkuk question the rationale of what God is doing, but Job goes beyond questioning to accusing. He has come to believe that his circumstances reflect irrational disorder and concludes that God must be the author of disorder. This has crossed a line. In the big picture of the world and our lives, God is surely to be seen as the one who is ultimately responsible for the adversity that we face (Eccl 7:14 affirms Job's sentiments to this effect as expressed in Job 1:21; 2:10). God's agency, however, does not make him the author of disorder. He has not eradicated it, but disorder does not flow from him.

A final indicator of flaws in Job's picture of God can be seen in his plea, "God weigh me in honest scales" (Job 31:6). Such a request should go without saying and implies that God might be inclined to the contrary. This puts us in the position of determining whether God is doing right. What is the standard for justice if it is not God himself? God cannot be appraised according to an outside standard, for that would make him contingent on that standard. With Job we must learn that it is not our place to hold God accountable. In fact, such a theological idea creates an oxymoron that intrinsically construes God as less than God.

JOB'S VIEW THAT GOD CAN BE MANIPULATED

Finally, Job has marginalized God such that God is now not only flawed but can be manipulated. Job had tried to engage God and failed, so now he uses him. Job no longer believes he will find justice from God; he now seeks some sort of coherence by attempting to regain equilibrium in society.

All of this—manipulation and search for equilibrium—is undertaken by means of Job's oath of innocence in Job 31. As Job enumerates all the offenses he has not committed, he is in effect inviting God to strike him dead if he actually *is* guilty of any of these crimes. Up until this time God's silence has been working against Job. God had presumably struck him, as anyone would infer, and his refusal to respond to Job's pleas, demands and accusations only reinforces the conclusion that Job is out of favor. Job now intends either to force God's hand by making him take action against Job or, more likely, to find vindication in God's silence. Job could then claim that his oath, and God's failure to act against him as one who has made a false oath, would show that he is indeed not guilty of any of those offenses. God's silence would tacitly, passively exonerate Job. Hypothetically Job might hope that he could therefore again stand tall among his peers as one who has done no wrong—his reputation sustained when no response from God is forthcoming. Some sort of equilibrium might therefore be restored for him in his social context.

Unfortunately there is some collateral damage here. If God's initial ruin of Job is proven unjustifiable, as would be demonstrated by Job's innocence in all the areas of his oath, God would be seen to be inconsistent in his policies. If God has no answer to give to Job's oath, it would demonstrate that he has ruined Job without cause, which would mean that Job's reputation is salvaged while God's is forfeit. Job's manipulative strategy is a tragic indicator of the cost Job is willing to pay to bring coherence to his world.

In the ritual vignette in Job 1:4-5, Job's behavior suggested that he believed God could be managed. He has progressed to believing that God can be outmaneuvered. In ritual approaches one may come to believe that God's picayune expectations can be addressed by meticulously meeting his needs. Job shows no indication that he considers God needy, but he has come to wonder whether God is apathetic, violent, preoccupied or perhaps even inept. Instead, God should be seen as attentive, compassionate, wise and beyond our attempts to manipulate.

The theology that Job maintains can be discerned from his speeches, and that theology is found wanting. This is not to criticize Job, because we all fall prey to the same misperceptions and false conclusions—particularly when we face trials. Because we are prone to the same ways of thinking, it is important to understand that the book is not sanctioning these ideas. Instead, the book exposes these distortions that are inimical to the true character of God.

FOR FURTHER REFLECTION

1. How do we distinguish Job's view of God from the author's?

2. What does Job think about God, and how are we to evaluate his portrait of the divine?

4

READING JOB

AS A CHRISTIAN

■   ■   ■

SEVENTEEN

JOB AND JESUS

Up to this point in the book, we have explored the meaning and message of the book of Job in its Old Testament setting without recourse to the New Testament. In other words, we have been reading the book as if we were among its ancient recipients. Of course to do so takes a measure of discipline and imagination since we don't live in the ancient world but rather more than two millennia after the book was first written and read.

It is critically important to read any Old Testament book in its original setting, which is why we have put such emphasis on reading the book of Job as the original audience would have received it. These books were written in order to address questions and concerns that were current at the time of composition and that still remain relevant for us today. God revealed himself to his people in terms that they could understand at the time, using language, metaphors, turns of phrases and genres that made sense to them. If we read an Old Testament book like Job too quickly from our twenty-first-century perspective, we run great risk of introducing meaning that wasn't intended by either the human or the divine author. By reading the New Testament back into the Old Testament, we also risk missing the rich theocentric (God-centered) meaning of the passage available to the Old Testament reader.

READING TWICE

But once we as Christians have read Job carefully from the perspective of its original setting, then we should read the book a second time in the light of the whole Bible, including the New Testament. After all, now Job appears in a broader context—the canon—and we need to read the book in light of the whole canon, including the New Testament. The New Testament gives us an inspired account of the continuation of the story of redemption that began in the book of Genesis; thus we can look back on the earlier story in the context of its continuation.

In principle we are encouraging a reading of the Bible that is not different from reading any other book or watching a movie, for that matter. Jon Levenson, a prominent Jewish academic, recognizes the importance for the Christian of reading the Old Testament in the light of the New Testament. He likens it to reading a Shakespeare play when he says, "Christian exegesis requires that the Hebrew Bible be read ultimately in a literary context that includes the New Testament. To read it only on its own would be like reading the first three acts of Hamlet as if the last two had never been written."[1]

To understand this principle, simply watch a good murder story on TV or in the movies twice. As you watch it the first time, you learn about characters and the facts of the case as the drama unfolds, then at the end the murderer is exposed. The second time you watch, the movie will be a different experience since you know how it ends.

The analogy is helpful because, according to the New Testament, Jesus is the fulfillment of the Old Testament message. We will cite just three passages to make our point.

First, in the opening chapter of John we read about how Jesus called Philip and Nathanael to follow him as his disciples. Philip was first, and he went to get his friend Nathanael and told him, "We have found the one Moses wrote about in the Law, and about whom the prophets also wrote—Jesus of Nazareth, the son of Joseph" (Jn 1:45). To understand what Philip is saying, we need to remember that at the time of Jesus and still today among Jewish readers the Old Testament was not the Old Testament. Rather it was often called "the Law and the Prophets." Here Philip comments that Jesus is anticipated in the Law and the Prophets, in other words in the entirety of the Old Testament.

We find this terminology as well as a close variant in the stories found in our second passage, Luke 24. This chapter records Jesus' actions and speeches during the time between his resurrection and his ascension. Luke records two meetings with different groups of disciples in this chapter, and, significantly, on both occasions Jesus speaks to them about the Law and the Prophets and in particular stresses the importance of reading it in the context of his coming.

The first encounter is with two disciples who are walking to the small village of Emmaus after the crucifixion of Jesus. These men are deeply discouraged, thinking that all the hopes they had placed in Jesus are now dashed. The resurrected Jesus then starts walking along with them, but they do not recognize him because God keeps them from doing so. He amazes them by asking them what makes them so downcast, but when they tell him it is because of the death of the object of their hope, he responds: "How foolish you are, and how slow to believe all that the prophets have spoken! Did not the Messiah have to suffer these things and then enter his glory?" And then Luke says that "beginning with Moses and all the Prophets, he explained to them what was said in all the Scriptures concerning himself" (Lk 24:25-27).

The second episode involves a larger group of disciples. To them he says, "'This is what I told you while I was still with you: Everything must be fulfilled that is written about me in the Law of Moses, the Prophets and the Psalms.' Then he opened their minds so they could understand the Scriptures" (Lk 24:44-45).

Jesus' point in these two encounters with his disciples was, to put it one way, to give them a lesson about the importance of interpreting the Old Testament from a Christian perspective. His frustration with their lack of understanding shows that they should have understood beforehand. But now that Christ has come, his presence in the Old Testament is all the more clear. To us living in the twenty-first century it is a call to read the Old Testament in the light of Christ's life, death and resurrection.

Our third and final passage indicates that Paul understood well the connection between Jesus and the Old Testament. For example, in his second letter to the Corinthians, he tells them, "For no matter how many promises God has made, they are 'Yes' in Christ" (2 Cor 1:20). God made lots of promises in the Old Testament, and Paul, as well as the other New Testament writers, understood that these promises found their ultimate fulfillment in Christ. One notable example, Galatians 3, shows that Paul understood that it was Jesus who was the ultimate fulfillment of the promise of "seed" to Abraham (see in particular Gal 3:16). This example could be multiplied many times.

These passages and others inform the Christian reader that it is not only permissible but important to read the Old Testament in the light of the New Testament. However, there are also certain risks involved, so it is important to do so carefully. Here are some guidelines:

1. As mentioned above, always begin by reading an Old Testament passage in its original setting before reading it from the perspective of the New Testament.

2. While Christ's relationship to the Old Testament is more than a matter of a handful of messianic prophecies (which themselves often have an Old Testament meaning apart from Christ), Christ is not to be found in every word, verse or chapter. Be careful of seeing Christ everywhere.

3. There must be an organic connection between the Old Testament meaning and its christological significance.

4. The New Testament itself will often cite the Old Testament and show a relationship to Christ. Even so we must be careful to realize that the connection is not always based on what we might call a historical-grammatical reading of the Old Testament text. Sometimes the New Testament treats the Old Testament text in ways that surprise us but are in keeping with first-century A.D. methods of interpretation.

5. Different books and even different parts of the same book may point to Christ in different ways.

6. As we will see with the book of Job and its teaching on wisdom, sometimes the connection to Christ is on a thematic level.

7. Of course, we can be fully confident when the New Testament's inspired authors make a connection with an Old Testament passage.

Otherwise we must admit a certain measure of uncertainty when we suggest a christological connection without New Testament precedent.

In sum, according to the teaching of the New Testament, the Old Testament anticipates the life and ministry of Jesus. Augustine captured the spirit of what we are saying when he stated, "The New Testament is in the Old Testament concealed; the Old is in the New revealed." When we read any part of the Old Testament, we must ask, how does this anticipate Christ? It is with that spirit that we turn our attention specifically to the book of Job. How does the book of Job anticipate Christ?

"I KNOW THAT MY REDEEMER LIVES!" (JOB 19:25)

George Frideric Handel's (1685–1759) rendition of Job 19:25 begins one of the most stirring arias of his powerful oratorio, *Messiah*. In this aria Jesus is the Redeemer. Is this, then, the sort of anticipation of Jesus that we are speaking about?

According to Walter Kaiser, the answer is yes. Indeed, he believes that all Job's appeals for a mediator between God and himself (Job 9:33; 16:19-21; 19:23-27; 33:23-28 [in this case, Elihu]) are messianic prophecies that anticipate Jesus.[2]

There are many problems with Kaiser's approach to these passages. He recognizes that there are a number of textual and interpretive issues, particularly with Job 19:23-27 (for which, see a fuller discussion in chap. 9), but he does not admit as he should that the best translation and understanding of the text do not support a messianic understanding. But no matter what the translation, a close look at the role of the hoped-for redeemer does not describe Jesus' future work.

A look at the relevant passages listed above indicates that Job wanted someone who would arbitrate between himself and God. He wanted someone to tell God to back off and to reconsider his unjust treatment of Job. God is being unfair in making him suffer in spite of the fact that he has done nothing wrong.

What is Job talking about when he talks about a mediator, an arbiter and a redeemer? We get our answer in Elihu's speech at the end of the book. In Job 33:23-28 Elihu speaks about the possibility that an angelic mediator could take up Job's case in heaven. Job certainly was hoping for the same. He hoped that an angel might take up his cause and intercede with God for him. The sad irony of his hope was that the only spiritual being taking up his case with God was the challenger, and as the reader knows—though Job did not—the challenger was advocating not for him but against him.

In addition there is a theological problem with the idea that Jesus is the arbiter, mediator or redeemer of Job in these passages. Job is looking for someone to mediate between him and God by calming God down. The New Testament indeed presents Jesus as the Mediator, indeed the only Mediator between God and his human creatures. But he wasn't working at cross-purposes with an angry God. Rather God the Father was the one who sent the Son to do his will by dying on the cross for the sins of those who turn to him (Mt 26:39).

Thus beginning with a well-known but, in our opinion, mistaken approach to seeing Jesus in the book of Job, we turn now to some more promising connections.

DO CHRISTIANS FEAR GOD FOR NOTHING?

The challenger's question ("Does Job fear God for nothing?" Job 1:9) is at the heart of the issue for the book of Job. Does Job worship and obey God for the good life that he lives, or does he love God because of who God is apart from the benefits? As God, through the agency of the challenger, removes his family, possessions and health, Job does not curse God and die. He does not turn his back on God but pursues him demanding an answer. And when God does make his presence known to him, Job responds by suffering in silence in the face of God's wisdom and power. The story indeed demonstrates that Job does fear God without expectation of benefits.

Reading the book as Christians, we should ask ourselves the same question. Why do we fear God? Do we love and obey Jesus for the benefits, or do we keep our focus on Jesus regardless of whether we live happy and enjoyable or difficult and painful lives?

Do Christians fear God? Before we answer this question we must address the question of whether God desires us to fear him. The question arises because one of the most beloved verses among Christians today is 1 John 4:18: "There is no fear in love. But perfect love drives out fear, because fear has to do with punishment. The one who fears is not made perfect in love."

We will return to this verse, but before we do we must take note that the New Testament often praises those who fear God and denigrates those who do not. We begin by citing Paul's admonition to "continue to work out your salvation with fear and trembling" (Phil 2:12). While Paul goes on to affirm the fact that God is sovereign in our salvation (Phil 2:13), he points out that our responsibility is to adopt an attitude of fear before God. Peter joins Paul in telling his Christian readers to "live out your time as foreigners here in reverent fear" (1 Pet 1:17; see also 1 Pet 2:17). These are just two of a number of passages that instruct Christians, just like their Old Testament counterparts, to "fear God" (see also Lk 1:50; 12:5; 23:40; Acts 9:31; 10:35; Rom 3:18; 2 Cor 5:11; 7:15; Rev 14:7; 19:5).

How do these admonitions to "fear God" fit in with John's statement that "there is no fear in love"? Obviously John is speaking of a fear other than the fear of God. He is speaking of the tendency we have to fear other people or to fear circumstances. In contrast, the fear of God that is commended in the Bible is that which indicates that we take God seriously in our lives and in our conduct. The opposite of fearing God in this way would be to consider God negligible, impotent, apathetic or indulgent. As early as the book of Deuteronomy, we see that there is no conflict between the fear of God and the love of God. In his final sermon before his death, Moses urges Israel "to fear the LORD your God, to walk in obedience to him, to love him, to serve the LORD your God with all your heart and with all your soul, and to observe the LORD's commands and decrees that I am giving you today for your own good" (Deut 10:12-13). Perfect love, which involves the fear of God, drives out those kinds of fears.

Do we fear God for nothing or for the goodies? With this background we now ask ourselves, why do we fear God? Do we fear him because he is God, or do we fear him because we think we will be rewarded for our relationship with him?

I remember that when I (Tremper) was a college student in the early 1970s a common evangelistic technique was to ask, do you want an abundant life? Different people probably meant different things by this question, but some meant, do you want an enjoyable life or a miserable one? Do you want a life of happiness or one of suffering? In other words, the appeal was to self-interest. What is in it for me? Of course, this is also the appeal of the so-called prosperity gospel, the idea that the life of faith results in health, wealth and happiness. And, while many of us resist the blatant self-interest of the prosperity gospel, we all at least from time to time will question what we did to deserve the negative things that happen in our lives.

But what does the New Testament promise us? Don't the authors of the New Testament appeal to us with the promise of an abundant life now and then address the threat of death with the promise of eternal life?

If we read the New Testament carefully, we see that God never promises that those who follow Jesus will live pain-free lives. Indeed the Christian disciple is one who will follow the example of the sufferings of Jesus and be willing to "take up the cross" of suffering in this life: "Whoever does not take up their cross and follow me is not worthy of me. Whoever finds their life will lose it, and whoever loses their life for my sake will find it" (Mt 10:38-39). The Christian life, according to Paul, is one of joy, but a joy in the midst of suffering. Paul speaks about his and others' "great endurance . . . hardships and distresses; in beatings, imprisonments and riots" (2 Cor 6:4-5) and more. He is "sorrowful, yet always rejoicing; poor, yet making many rich; having nothing, and yet possessing everything" (2 Cor 6:10). Paul models proper discipleship, which is a relationship with God, not for the goodies but because of his love of God. In this Paul and the obedient Christian disciples follow the example of Jesus himself,

Who, being in very nature God,
    did not consider equality with God something to be used to his
      own advantage;
rather, he made himself nothing
    by taking the very nature of a servant,

being made in human likeness.
And being found in appearance as a man,
  he humbled himself
  by becoming obedient to death—
    even death on a cross! (Phil 2:6-8)

We return to this topic at the very end of the book ("Disinterested righteousness," beginning on p. 166).

WHO IS WISE?

Another major concern of the book of Job is wisdom. One way of understanding the book is to see it as a debate about who has wisdom. Job's suffering provides the occasion for the debate. He has a serious problem that needs solving. Why is Job suffering, and what is the solution to his suffering?

Wisdom in the Bible begins with the practical skill of living. A wise person is one who knows how to navigate life in a way that will maximize success and minimize problems. Success may be defined as living a happy life, with a well-functioning family and with sufficient resources to enjoy life. The book of Proverbs gives advice that wise people will heed in order to achieve such a blessed life. When wise people fall into trouble, wisdom can help them get themselves out of the pit in which they have fallen. In many ways, at least on this level, wisdom is similar to what we call emotional intelligence.[3] A wise person knows the right thing to say at the right time as well as the right action for the situation. Timing is everything in wisdom. When it comes to Job's suffering, the wise person should be able to give the proper advice for Job to get out of his predicament.

In the earlier part of the book, we have recounted how each of the human characters of the book has presented himself as a wise person, claiming to be able to diagnose Job's problem and provide a proper remedy. The three friends repeatedly claim that Job's problem is the result of his sin, so he must repent. Job himself, believing that the retribution principle should work but hasn't in his case, concludes that God is unjust. Therefore his solution or remedy is to confront God and set him straight. Elihu, representing a claim to wisdom based on spiritual inspiration rather than age, also believes that Job's problem is his sin, though Elihu places more emphasis on the remedial rather than the punishing aspect of suffering.

As we review all these human pretensions to wisdom, we see that they all fall short. None of them get it right. We know right from the start that Job is not suffering because of his sin or because God is unjust. Therefore all their diagnoses and remedies are deeply flawed. Only God is truly wise, and that is his point when he confronts Job from the whirlwind in Job 38–42, a conclusion that is anticipated in Job 28 and that is recognized by Job when he sees rather than simply hears Yahweh. As a result, in the midst of suffering Job submits to the wisdom and power of Yahweh (Job 42:1-6).

As we read Job with its focus on wisdom, what does the New Testament contribute to the discussion? In short we learn that Jesus, the Son of God, is the very epitome of God's wisdom. When confronted with the question of where to find wisdom, the Christian answers "in a relationship with Jesus."

As we read through the Gospels, we see that Jesus is wise from the very beginning of his life. We don't hear much about Jesus as a young boy, but Luke informs us that "the child grew and became strong; he was filled with wisdom, and the grace of God was on him" (Lk 2:40). Luke makes a similar statement in Luke 2:52, and between these two verses is a story that illustrates Jesus' profound wisdom even at a young age: When Jesus was twelve, his parents took him to the temple for Passover, but as they returned, they realized that he had not left Jerusalem with them. Likely panicked, they returned to Jerusalem and finally found him sitting with the teachers of the temple. Luke comments that "everyone who heard him was amazed at his understanding and his answers" (Lk 2:47).

Not surprisingly, when Jesus came of age and began to teach, people were amazed with his wisdom. He was unique among the teachers of the law (Mk 1:22). Indeed "the people were all so amazed that they asked each other, 'What is this? A new teaching—and with authority! He even gives orders to impure spirits and they obey him'" (Mk 1:27). It is also significant that Jesus typically taught in the form of the parable. The English word *parable* translates the Greek term *parabolē,* which is also the Greek equivalent to *proverb* (*mashal*), the primary literary form of the wise teacher. In brief, the parable was the teaching vehicle of the sage. Jesus was the sage par excellence.[4]

Paul too affirms the deep, divine wisdom of Jesus. For Paul, Christ is "the power of God and the wisdom of God" (1 Cor 1:24). He is the one "in whom are hidden all the treasures of wisdom and knowledge" (Col 2:3).

Indeed the New Testament authors identify him, and Jesus identifies himself, with the figure of Woman Wisdom in the book of Proverbs. Woman Wisdom, as developed in the first part of the book of Proverbs (see Prov 1:20-33, especially Prov 8:1-36; 9:1-6), is the personification of Yahweh's wisdom and ultimately stands for Yahweh himself.[5]

In his response to Jewish leaders who question his rather celebratory lifestyle, Jesus associates himself with Woman Wisdom by telling them that "wisdom is proved right by her deeds" (Mt 11:19). Colossians 1:15-17 uses the language of Proverbs 8 when it describes Jesus as

> the image of the invisible God, the firstborn over all creation. For in him all things were created: things in heaven and on earth, visible and invisible, whether thrones or powers or rulers or authorities; all things have been created through him and for him. He is before all things, and in him all things hold together.

The majestic opening of the Gospel of John also echoes the language describing Woman Wisdom when it speaks of Christ as the Logos:

> In the beginning was the Word, and the Word was with God, and the Word was God. He was with God in the beginning. Through him all things were made; without him nothing was made that has been made. In him was life, and that life was the light of all mankind. (Jn 1:1-4)

Jesus is the very epitome of God's wisdom. Jesus is the answer to the question of where we find wisdom. When the book of Job asserts the wisdom of God, the Christian understands that Jesus displays God's wisdom in all its abundance. As we seek the wisdom of God rather than our own or any human wisdom, we are brought into an intimate relationship with our divine teacher.

WHAT IS THE RIGHTEOUSNESS GOD DESIRES?

As we look closely at the message of the book of Job, we see, as we argued earlier, that the book of Job is more about understanding righteousness (its nature and motives) than about understanding suffering. As we consider the book's message from the perspective of the New Testament, we are drawn to its teaching about the nature of true righteousness. According to the New Testament, what does true righteousness look like?

In short, true righteousness looks like Jesus (Acts 3:14; 1 Cor 1:30; 1 Jn 2:1, 29). He is sinless and keeps the law, following God's will perfectly. He embodies "faithfulness, justice, uprightness, correctness, loyalty, blamelessness, purity, salvation, and innocence."[6]

God desires us to be righteous like Jesus, but we are sinners and fall far short of God's standard of righteousness (Rom 3:23). We can't be righteous on our own power. Thus in his Sermon on the Mount Jesus tells us that we are to seek his righteousness (Mt 6:33).

Thank God we can be righteous by placing our trust in Jesus and participating in his righteousness. As Paul puts it,

> God presented Christ as a sacrifice of atonement, through the shedding of his blood—to be received by faith. He did this to demonstrate his righteousness, because in his forbearance he had left the sins committed beforehand unpunished—he did it to demonstrate his righteousness at the present time, so as to be just and the one who justifies those who have faith in Jesus. (Rom 3:25-26; see also Phil 3:7-11)

What does true righteousness look like? Jesus. How do we become righteous? Through our relationship with Jesus and in the power of the Holy Spirit, we strive to conform our thinking and actions to imitate him.

JOB AND JESUS AS INNOCENT SUFFERERS

Why did Job suffer? Did he deserve the pain he experienced?

Right from the start of the book, the reader of the book of Job knows that Job is not suffering because of his sin. From that perspective he did not deserve the suffering that came to him. He is in this regard truly an innocent sufferer.

As we survey the rest of the Old Testament, we find no other truly innocent sufferer. Daniel suffered by being taken to Babylon against his will. We do not learn of any personal sin that led to the hardship of his life, but we are not told, as we are with Job, that his suffering is unrelated to his sin. Daniel, it is evident, suffers because of the corporate sin of the people of Judah.

Again, Job is the one clear example of an innocent sufferer in the Old Testament. As we turn to the New Testament, we recognize only one other innocent sufferer, and that is Jesus. Jesus was without sin. He may have been tempted just as we are, "yet he did not sin" (Heb 4:15). Though he did not sin, he suffered throughout his life and died a horrible death by crucifixion. The early Christian community saw this connection between Job and Jesus, so it was a common practice to read the book of Job during Passion Week.[7]

Though such a comparison is fair, the similarity between Job and Jesus just highlights the important differences between them. In the first place, Job suffered involuntarily while Jesus suffered voluntarily. Job had no say over his pain, and when it afflicted him he complained and wanted to confront God and accuse him of injustice. Jesus struggled against his life of pain and his anticipated violent death to be sure. In the Garden of Gethsemane he asked God to take "this cup," the cup of suffering, "from me," but in the end he freely submitted himself to his Father's plan: "Yet not as I will, but as you will" (Mt 26:39).

Thus while Job had no choice regarding his suffering, Jesus submitted freely, and this leads us to the second contrast. Jesus voluntarily suffered on our behalf. In other words, Jesus suffered in our place for our sins so we can be reconciled with God. Jesus' suffering was redemptive; Job's was not. Job's suffering does not lead to the forgiveness of our sins or a new relationship with God. Job's suffering has a didactic purpose. As we read the story of his suffering and interaction with God, we learn important lessons about how our relationship with God (primarily that it should not be about the rewards) and about the wisdom and power of God.

JESUS: GOD'S ULTIMATE ANSWER TO OUR SUFFERING

The book of Job is disturbing to many readers because it does not answer the question of human suffering. Certainly Job suffers deeply in the book, and many people who deal with the pain of life find themselves attracted to the book of Job. But the book of Job is not about suffering. If we want to find out why there is suffering in the world and pain in our lives, the book of Job is not going to answer those questions.

The Bible as a whole speaks of many different possible reasons for suffering: We might suffer because of our sin. We might suffer because another person sinned. We might suffer because the world is broken. We might suffer like the man born blind (Jn 9:1-3) so that God might be glorified. There are a number of reasons why we might suffer loss, sickness or any other painful situation. Sometimes, as is the case with Job, we simply cannot know why we suffer.

In sum, the book of Job does not answer the question of why we suffer. It does not address God's response to our suffering. We do not turn to the book of Job to discover God's ultimate answer to our suffering; we turn to the New Testament, and there we see Jesus (for more, see "The Theology of Suffering in the Book of Job," chap. fifteen, p. 137).

As celebrated in Philippians 2:6-8 (quoted above), Jesus came into the world to suffer and even to die on the cross. Paul elsewhere (Gal 3:10-13) and Peter (1 Pet 2:21-25 and 3:18) describe this death as punishment for our sin. We deserve to die, but he dies in our place. But because he suffered in our place, he was also glorified. The passage from Philippians continues:

> Therefore God exalted him to the highest place
> and gave him the name that is above every name,
> that at the name of Jesus every knee should bow,
> in heaven and on earth and under the earth,
> and every tongue acknowledge that Jesus Christ is Lord,
> to the glory of God the Father. (Phil 2:9-11)

FOR FURTHER REFLECTION

1. Summarize the main connections made in this chapter between Job

and the New Testament. Evaluate each. Can you think of any others?

2. What do Jesus' comments about the relationship between him and the Old Testament ("the Law . . . the Prophets and the Psalms," Lk 24:44) tell us about the continuing importance of the Old Testament for Christians today?

EIGHTEEN

THE MESSAGE OF THE
BOOK OF JOB FOR TODAY

As we have seen, the book of Job is more challenging than most books of the Bible. It does not yield its truths in a straightforward manner. Its affirmations have to be excavated from all the claims made throughout the book that themselves show varying levels of fallacy. As is true throughout the Bible, the message is ultimately about God.

The most dangerous falsehoods are those that are closest to the truth. Their subtlety makes them insidious as they infiltrate our thinking. We are particularly prone to misconstrue God because, even though we are in his image, he is not like us. Yet it is our inclination to reshape him in our own image. We tend to be suspicious of him because he is other and because he has power over us. We know well how power corrupts us, so it is easy for us to imagine that it corrupts God as well. We are also prone to misconceptions because we wonder whether God is attentive enough and whether he cares enough. These are issues that will be addressed in the following discussions.

DOES THE BOOK OF JOB PROVIDE ANSWERS?

In order to address whether the book provides answers, we need to clarify what questions are on the table. For most people the question that they want answered is why. The book deftly disassembles all the familiar answers that perpetually circulate. In chapter three we enumerated some of the answers offered in the ancient Near East to explain the suffering of those who appeared innocent and pious, and these are not dissimilar to those that people still hold today:

- No sinless child has been born.
- Gods have made people with evil inclinations and prone to suffering.
- Gods are inscrutable since they are inconsistent and unpredictable.
- The purposes of the gods are remote.

We will deal with each one in turn.

No sinless child has been born. This is, of course, true, but it does not offer an explanation for why the innocent suffer. If our sin caused our suffering, then we all should be suffering all the time, and we should be suffering for our sin and not the sins of others. In the ancient Near East there were many ways to offend the gods, but the gods were not consistent in their responses. It was never clear why they would take umbrage at some rather insignificant infractions and other fairly major trespasses would pass unnoticed.

Readers of the Bible sometimes wonder why Nadab and Abihu (Lev 10) or Achan (Josh 7) or Uzzah (2 Sam 6) was treated so harshly when others remained unscathed. We may well wonder, but finding God arbitrary is not one of the options. Our belief in the authority of the Bible requires that we submit to the coherent picture of God that it offers. If something seems not to fit, it is because of our limited understanding. God gets the benefit of the doubt. Always.

We know that inherent sinfulness is not the answer the book promulgates because the text makes it clear throughout that Job is considered righteous. That does not mean that he is perfect, but he is above reproach in his conduct. Furthermore God affirms that he has ruined Job without cause (Job 2:3). No one is without sin, but we cannot just pull out that theological fact as a trump card when we try to understand our human plight.

God made us with evil inclinations and prone to suffer. This was one answer given in the ancient world, and the biblical understanding sought to counter this common assumption. God did not make people with evil inclinations. Our evil inclinations are the result of attempting to make ourselves the center of wisdom and order. This is human nature in the post-fall world, and it accounts for our evil inclinations (Gen 8:21).

God *did*, however, make us prone to suffering, in a manner of speaking. As we discussed earlier, we are vulnerable to suffering because we live in a world that is both unfinished (non-order) and corrupt (disorder). These circumstances mean that we are prone to suffering. Yet that is not the explanation the book offers for Job's suffering or ours. It may offer perspective on why there is suffering in the world, but it does not answer why one person suffers and another does not. It does not explain why some people have lives that are filled with suffering while others live carefree lives.

God is inscrutable, inconsistent and unpredictable. The God of the Bible may at times be unpredictable, but he is not inconsistent. The former statement simply recognizes that his plan is bigger than any of us can imagine. The latter reflects our theological conviction that God always acts consistently with his character, complex as it is. Unlike the gods of the ancient world (and unfortunately at times like the god of our imagination), who may reflect certain attributes one day and be totally different the next, the God of the Bible is characterized by attributes that always operate in harmony.

We may agree that God is inscrutable in the sense that he cannot be fully known, but in the book of Job it is God's reasons that are beyond our knowing and beyond our ability to infer. Job is never told why he suffered. Even the prologue does not offer a potential reason for suffering (a bet with the devil). The narrative scenario does not offer a reason; it sets the scene and in doing so indicates there is no reason. If Job were given a reason, the situation would cease to be realistic. The argument against inscrutability is that we need not seek answers that will justify Job's or our experiences; we know enough to believe that God is wise.

God's purpose is remote. It is difficult to argue with this in the main, but it is truer of the gods of the ancient Near East than it is of Yahweh because Yahweh has revealed himself to and through Israel. Certainly

God's revelation can only unveil what we are capable of understanding, but one of the key aspects of that revelation pertains to the broad spectrum of his plan, his overarching purposes. Nothing of that sort exists in the ancient Near East. There the conduct of the gods is more ad hoc. It is true that in the biblical view the depth of God's wisdom is unfathomable, the understanding of his judgments unsearchable and his paths beyond tracing (Rom 11:33). He is transcendent, far above us in every way. But the thrust of this proposed explanation is that there *are* divine purposes that would explain our experiences. That is not the sort of answer the book offers.

When we look to the past, we are seeking reasons. When we look to the future, we are seeking purposes. The former attempt should be abandoned and the latter held loosely. We should not seek reasons for our suffering because we have no basis for thinking that they exist. If some of our experiences result from living in a world that includes non-order and disorder, then those experiences are not the result of reasons. In contrast, we *can* seek out purposes for our suffering, but there is no guarantee that we will find them, and purposes can be complex. For example, consider the tragic situation in which a loved one is in a car accident, survives in a coma for a few days and then dies. We would have no basis for declaring that such an incident had a purpose for that person. Nevertheless, that tragedy may serve purposes in the lives of loved ones and friends. The point is that when we suffer, we can look for purposes and often find them, but at other times any purpose may be elusive. Regardless, we can be confident that everything that happens is folded into God's purposes. These purposes may indeed be remote, but this is a very different level of discussion than that with which we began.

OTHER QUESTIONS AND ANSWERS

Besides the question of why bad things happen to good people, readers often want answers about what God is doing. They are convinced that he has a lot to answer for. This is closer to the question that the book is posing (concerning God's policies). But don't expect God to defend himself. If we ask why God runs the world the way that he does, we have put our finger on the pulse of the book. But the answer the book provides is basically, as the saying goes, above our pay grade. That does not mean that God pulls rank with a blanket dismissal, "I'm God, you're not." It is more like, "I am God, trust my wisdom." That may sound great, but it often strikes those who are suffering as woefully inadequate. We are baffled by what sort of wisdom could possibly allow genocide, starvation, congenital diseases or horrific accidents. But isn't that where trust comes in? If we could work it all out, there would be no need for trust.

The book definitely wants to address another question that people don't often ask: Is there such a thing as disinterested righteousness? That is, does *anyone* serve God for nothing? This gets to the heart of the question of what defines our faith. Is our religion more than a way to achieve what we believe to be beneficial outcomes? We will address this further in the last chapter, but here we ask whether the book gives an answer to this question, and we find that it does. Job demonstrates that his service to God is not driven by the expectation of gain. His motivations are not selfish, and his commitments are not conditional.

So, in summary, what answers *does* the book provide?

- Beyond the fact that we do not get an explanation of *why* something happened, the book helps us to arrive at the important insight that we should not think that there *is* an explanation. In other words, it is not just a case that there is an answer that we simply cannot know because we cannot comprehend it or because it is being withheld.

- We cannot out-God God. We must not permit ourselves the illusion that, given the reins of the world, we could do it better. Such mistaken thinking puts us precisely in Job's shoes, thinking too simplistically and mechanically about God and thinking too highly of ourselves.

- Trust is the only possible response. Our experiences are beyond explanation. Reasons are fleeting and inadequate. The worse the situation is, the harder it is to trust and the more it is necessary to do so.

- God's wisdom prevails; God's justice is to be affirmed but cannot be expected to be evident in our experiences.

- Our benefits must be devalued in our minds. Our relationship with God is foremost. What we get out of it is valued but must not be the driving force in our commitments and behavior.

FOR FURTHER REFLECTION

1. Before reading this book, what kind of questions did you think the book of Job would or did answer?

2. In your own words describe the questions that the book of Job does answer.

3. How helpful are the answers of Job for your life?

NINETEEN

DOES THE BOOK OF
JOB PROVIDE COMFORT?

To begin to address this question, we first need to ask, what do we mean when we talk about being comforted? We know that it doesn't help for someone to tell us it's OK or everything will be fine. Those are typically hollow words. In fact many of the clichés that are bandied about glibly when people are suffering represent well-intentioned attempts to offer comfort. We might feel comforted if someone were able to tell us that something we feared (e.g., a report that the biopsy showed malignancy) would not materialize. Again, that is more relief than comfort. Sometimes we might be comforted in the death of a loved one when we are told, "They didn't suffer—it was a peaceful death." Again, the comfort derives from information that tells us that the situation was not as bad as it could have been or that things will definitely get better.

How could Job have been comforted? Would he have been comforted if, rather than turning against him, his friends had commiserated with him, affirming his victim status and sadly shaking their heads at his clearly undeserved misfortune? We may find momentary solace in the company of those who can help shoulder the burden of our suffering, but that comfort is fleeting. Would he have been comforted if Yahweh had told him about the scene in heaven and explained that he was a pawn in a high-stakes confrontation of epic proportions? More likely he would have found that as discomforting as many readers do. The outrageousness of that scenario would multiply his discomfort and dissatisfaction. Would he have been comforted if God had made known to him a cause-and-effect connection (since the retribution principle had led people to believe that such connections must exist)? Such knowledge could result in someone being resigned to an unfortunate situation but may lead more to self-recrimination than to comfort. When people with type 2 diabetes learn that all their years of reckless overindulgence in food that sent carbohydrates surging through their circulation systems may have contributed to their current health crises, the explanation is more likely to stimulate guilt than comfort.

Was Job comforted when his prosperity was restored and life returned to normal? It is interesting to note that *after* his restoration, his relatives and friends came to dine at his house and "comforted and consoled him over all the trouble the LORD had brought on him" (Job 42:11). Great! *Now* they show up! And they gave him silver and a gold ring. What comfort is that? In a real-life situation we would recognize that no restoration would return his dead children to him. When he suddenly enjoyed blessing again, he was more comfortable, but that is not the same as being comforted. Confusion more likely results. We can imagine him saying, "What was that all about?" Finally, was Job comforted to hear God say to the friends, "You have not spoken the truth about me, as my servant Job has" (Job 42:7)? Do compliments bring comfort? Anyone would revel in someday hearing, "Well done, good and faithful servant" (Mt 25:21), but how would Job assess this accolade from God? He could conclude that he had responded passably (he can't be too encouraged by that; we recall that he has already been sharply reprimanded for aspects of his responses), but that does not make everything that had happened go away or make sense. Job received no comfort from his friends, from Yahweh or from answers he received. Even when he returned to prosperity, he found relief but no comfort.

Does the book of Job provide comfort for us? When understood in the way that we have discussed above, the short answer, of course, is no—and it is not designed to do so. Reading the book will not make us feel better about our own crises. In fact it is a hard book to read for someone who is suffering. When I learn of a friend or loved one who has entered some sort of crisis through loss or illness, my first response is not to tell them they should read the book of Job for comfort. The message of the book is more suited to training for crises than to performing in a crisis.

As an illustration, the training required by a concert pianist includes spending hours each day rehearsing scales and performing finger exercises, as well as practicing the concert repertoire over and over. The scales are not going to be part of the concert, but they are the fundamentals on which every piece is based. The finger exercises maintain the flexibility to execute difficult sequences, preparing the pianist for the challenges that must be faced to render a beautiful performance. The endless practicing of the pieces insures that when it comes time for the performance, the master pianist will be able to let instinct take over—the fingers have learned what they need to do. I (John) once heard the great Christian educator Howard Hendricks tell the story of having the opportunity to meet the renowned pianist Van Cliburn: "I asked him a question I had wondered about for years: 'How many hours a day do you practice?' He told me matter-of-factly, 'Six to eight hours—with at least two hours of finger exercises.' I then remembered how I once wanted to play the piano—but never that badly!"

Some of us would like results but are not willing to put in the hard work necessary to achieve those results. The book of Job provides the opportunity for training our minds to maintain spiritual flexibility and to act instinctively when the need arises. We shouldn't start learning scales the day of the performance, and we should not think that we can sight-read a challenging score once the concert has begun. The lessons of Job should be learned in preparation for crises, not turned to for comfort after life has gone desperately wrong.

COMFORT OR ACCEPTANCE?

We would recommend an alternative to using the book of Job to find or give comfort and hopefully a purpose that is ultimately more satisfying: acceptance. Acceptance is found in gaining a revised perspective on our pain or suffering—something that helps us to think about ourselves and our situation in different terms and to see God in new light.

Our distress in suffering is the result of a combination of factors: fear, pain, grief, anxiety and uncertainty all contribute to the feeling that everything is out of kilter and beyond our control. But these psychological factors are compounded by spiritual ones. Perhaps we worry that our past sins (known or unknown) are catching up with us. Perhaps we come to wonder whether God is less than we thought. Physical crises can often be compounded by a crisis of faith.

The book of Job offers relief from the quest for explanations and from the suspicion that God has let us down or even become our enemy. This will not reduce pain or resolve our grief. But it may ease some of our fear and anxiety. Perhaps most importantly it can address the question of control.

When we recognize most clearly that we are not in control, we want to believe that someone is in control and in that belief to find hope. Those who enjoy riding roller coasters revel in the feeling of danger that they experience during the ride, the sensation of being out of control. Even the most avid aficionado of roller-coaster thrills, however, would be reticent to ride a roller coaster that truly was out of control—jumping the tracks and killing all on board several times each day. We do not want our lives to feel like that. Even when we realize we are not in control, we would like to have some reassurance that God is.

The book of Job helps us to understand the terms of God's control and what that should lead us to expect or not expect. The retribution principle had made it easy—righteous people should expect prosperity and a life free of suffering. That is *too* easy. God's control of the cosmos and of our lives is not like that. He has created the world to work the way that it does, and he does not step in every time one of his faithful ones is threatened. Nothing is outside of his control, but as we have discussed previously he does not imprint his justice on the cosmos. Control should not be defined as micromanagement. If we can accept this view of God's role in the world, our expectations of him can be revised and we can accept the circumstances that come upon us with more resolve. If we really believe that God is wise and we are not, then we can reliquish control to him in spite of our lack of understanding. We should not expect to find comfort in explanations, but acceptance of the way God made the world to work and acceptance that what we experience is not in vain can give us hope and a reason to trust. Such acceptance can be discussed in terms of rest, *shalom* and coherence.

REST

Rest in the biblical sense is not the opposite of activity; it is the opposite of unrest. This unrest can be the result of either non-order (when natural disasters strike) or of disorder (when violence threatens our lives and communities). Rest is the result of order. It is characterized by stability and security. Exodus 20:11 reports that God took up his rest when he had completed his work of creation. Psalm 132:8, 13-14 identifies the temple as God's resting place. From there he brings order and stability to his people, indeed, to the cosmos. From there he rules (Ps 132:14), and among the outcomes of that rule are his care for the people of Israel (Ps 132:15) and the success of the king (Ps 132:17-18). God's presence and rule are central to having a stable community.

God promises to bring rest to his people as they enter the land of Canaan to claim their covenant inheritance. Deuteronomy 12:10 makes it clear that when God gives his people rest from their enemies, they will "live in safety" (cf. Ex 33:14; Josh 1:13-15; 21:44). God also accomplishes this for David (2 Sam 7:1, 11) and for Solomon (1 Kings 5:4; cf. also Asa, 2 Chron 14:6-7, and Jehoshaphat, 2 Chron 20:30). The Jews of Esther's time were also given rest (Esther 9:22), and rest characterizes God's restoration of Israel (Is 14:1-3; 32:18; Ezek 37:14), which explicitly involves relief from suffering and turmoil. We can see then that rest is applied to a condition of stability and security that God achieves on the society level.

But rest is not just something God achieves for the covenant community. When Naomi sends Orpah and Ruth back to their families, it is with the blessing that they might find rest with another husband (Ruth 1:8-9). This rest refers to a personal level of stability and security within a community. The wise woman who brings a story to David, in which she might lose both her sons, requests that he take action to assure that her inheritance be secured (2 Sam 14:17).

We can define rest as pertaining to the stability and security God brings to a community or that an individual finds within a community. When the book of Job begins, Job has rest. He has a secure role in a community in which he is respected. He loses that status (described most fully in Job 30), strategizes to regain it (Job 31) and eventually does so (Job 42). Nevertheless, the noun for "rest" never occurs in the book of Job, and the verb occurs only three times, all in Job's lament (Job 3:13, 17, 26), where the only rest that he can anticipate is in death.

Job's hopelessness is paralleled in a final Old Testament example. In Jeremiah's oracle to his scribe, Baruch, it is instructive to learn that Baruch's sorrow, pain and groaning will continue and he will "find no rest" (Jer 45:1-5). The cases of Job and Baruch make it clear that suffering threatens rest. So how can an individual hope to achieve rest in the midst of suffering?

The New Testament offers us another dynamic at work in the idea of rest. Jesus is addressing a familiar theological topic when he invites his listeners, "Come to me, all you who are weary and burdened, and I will give you rest. Take my yoke upon you and learn from me, for I am gentle and humble in heart, and you will find rest for your souls. For my yoke is easy and my burden is light" (Mt 11:28-30). In these verses we have moved beyond the circumstances of the stability of society, beyond the security of a family and beyond personal comfort to a consideration of rest at an entirely different level: "rest for your souls." This rest is given by Jesus as he adjusts their perspective to that which is appropriate to disciples in the kingdom of God. The rest we find in Jesus is not in an earthly community but in the community that is the kingdom of God.

We conclude this brief summary of the biblical theology of rest by noting the discussion of it in Hebrews 3–4. Hebrews 4:1 informs us that "the promise of entering his rest still stands," and "we who have believed enter that rest" (Heb 4:3). Yet the author of Hebrews exhorts his readers to "make every effort to enter that rest" (Heb 4:11). The rest discussed in Hebrews, like that addressed by Christ, refers to the stability and security

found in the kingdom of God, where our perspective is a heavenly perspective, not an earthly one.

On the basis of this biblical investigation, we can now understand that
rest is what we seek when we are undergoing times of crisis or suffering.
A community can experience unrest when it is experiencing trouble
within society (crime, repression), when it is experiencing threats from
people outside (invasions, persecution) or when it is experiencing
catastrophe (famine, devastation from natural disasters). Individuals
experience unrest when they are cut off from their community—despised
or rejected.

The mistake that is evident in the Old Testament and still too often
exists today happens when a community, having adopted the retribution
principle, believes that someone who is suffering must deserve punishment. This belief leads a community to ostracize the suffering person.
The Christian way is different. We should rally around the person who is
suffering. When that happens people can find rest even in their suffering
as they find support and security in a stable community.

Furthermore, even if we do not find rest for our minds or bodies, Christ
calls us to lay our burdens on him and find rest for our souls. The Christian
perspectives are important for us, but the book of Job does not go this far;
it has no such hope to offer. Job does not find rest in the midst of his suffering; only after he is restored does he find rest. Our hope for rest is found
in Christ and in the community of the church; Job does not take us there.
The only stability the book has to offer in times of suffering is that which
comes from trust in God's wisdom, not human wisdom.

SHALOM

What is the difference between *rest* and *shalom*? They are rarely used together in the Old Testament or to explain each other. Nevertheless, the
description of *shalom* in Leviticus 26:6 would be difficult to distinguish
from the description of rest: "I will grant peace [*shalom*] in the land, and
you will lie down and no one will make you afraid. I will remove wild
beasts from the land, and the sword will not pass through your country."
As another example, 1 Kings 4:24 reports that God gave Solomon *shalom*

on all sides, and in 1 Kings 5:3-4 Solomon notes that God has given him rest on every side. In 1 Chronicles 22:9 God will give Solomon rest as well as "peace and quiet." Jeremiah 14:19 associates *shalom* with healing:

> Have you rejected Judah completely?
>   Do you despise Zion?
> Why have you afflicted us
>   so that we cannot be healed?
> We hoped for peace
>   but no good has come,
> for a time of healing
>   but there is only terror.

The term *shalom* occurs only four times in the book of Job. Eliphaz speaks of a situation in which one has lost no property and therefore his tent is *shalom* (Job 5:24, NIV "secure"). He also envisions the fate of the wicked as a situation when even at the moment he feels like he is safe (*shalom*) from torment, marauders attack (Job 15:21). In Job's estimation a home that is free from fear and God's punishment is characterized as *shalom* (Job 21:9). In the final occurrence, Bildad asserts that God is the one who established *shalom* in the heavens (Job 25:2, NIV "order").

God is the one who gives both rest and *shalom*. Rest is more than *shalom*, but if there is no *shalom*, there cannot be rest. *Shalom* has to do with wellness and well-being (at a variety of levels). It can refer to the absence of war or strife, but it can also refer to prosperity and everything being in order. Our bodies may or may not be well, yet in either situation we may be able to affirm that "it is well with my soul." *Shalom* is best understood as a feeling (whether realistic or not) that all is well. Consequently, even when we are in crisis and are experiencing significant unrest, we can feel *shalom*.

Again, the New Testament adds some important perspectives as we observe its use of the Greek equivalent of *shalom*, generally rendered "peace." In John 14:27 Jesus tells his disciples in the upper room, "Peace I leave with you; my peace I give you. I do not give to you as the world gives. Do not let your hearts be troubled and do not be afraid." Here we can see that Christ is the source of peace and that peace is the opposite of fear. Later in the discussion Jesus is trying to reassure his disciples that their grief will turn to joy (Jn 16:20-22) and concludes with "I have told you these things, so that in me you may have peace. In this world you will have trouble. But take heart! I have overcome the world" (Jn 16:33). Peace can be the feeling that all is well even when circumstances are difficult.

Paul's usage demonstrates that the Greek term crosses semantic lines since he also employs "peace" as the opposite of unrest (1 Cor 14:33) when he addresses disruptions within the community. In Ephesians 2:11-22, the classic passage on reconciliation of communities to one another and to God through Christ, we are called to remember that when we were separate from Christ, we were excluded foreigners without hope (Eph 2:12). Nevertheless, in Christ we are no longer ostracized, having been brought near by the blood of Christ. Paul then reaches a climax as he proclaims,

> For he himself is our peace, who has made the two groups [Jew and Gentile] one and has destroyed the barrier, the dividing wall of hostility. . . . His purpose was to create in himself one new humanity out of the two, thus making peace, and in one body to reconcile both of them to God through the cross, by which he put to death their hostility. He came and preached peace to you who were far away and peace to those who were near. (Eph 2:14-17)

In these verses Paul merges the idea of feeling that all is well with that of stability of community and shows both to be accomplished by the work of Christ. The result is a community that is more than a human community; it is the kingdom of God on earth.

On the foundation of this study, we need to return now to the book of Job and our responses to it. Job does not feel *shalom* at any time throughout his crisis, and even his response to Yahweh's speeches does not show any progress on that matter. He expresses his feelings of unworthiness and ignorance, and humbles himself before God. He has set aside his self-confidence and his self-righteousness, but fear and disenfranchisement remain unaffected.

But what about us? Is the book of Job supposed to help us resolve our fears and find *shalom*? Insofar as a feeling of *shalom* can be experienced through trust and acceptance even while the crisis is ongoing, we should answer in the affirmative. When fear subsides, *shalom* is the result. Job did not fear death, though sometimes we do. Job did not fear pain, though he did not welcome it (nor do we). Job did not have peace because he did not have rest. Jesus still says "fear not" as well as "I will give you rest." In this, Jesus has given us a focus for our trust—far more focus than Job had. In this way the book of Job starts us on a journey of trust and hope that finds its completion in Christ.

COHERENCE

By coherence we refer to a situation in which we have been able to put the pieces together so that our experience is comprehensible. It is not the same as having all the answers or knowing what will happen. Rather, coherence indicates that we have achieved an optimum level of understanding. When we lack coherence, both rest and *shalom* are jeopardized. Job was seeking some level of coherence as he attempted to call God into court and as he made his oath of innocence. In the book as a whole, however, we get no sense that Job achieves coherence. His responses to Yahweh's speeches give no such indication, and any coherence he achieves in his restoration would not address our concerns—the book does not suggest that our crises will be resolved.

Yet somehow the book does point us in the direction of finding coherence. As we recall the speeches of Yahweh, the first reminds us how complex God's work in the world is and that it is not a world that he has harnessed to perform according to his attributes. Job accepts these truths. In the second speech, the lesson of Behemoth teaches us that Job (and we) should be steadfast and immovable in the strong currents of life. The lesson of Leviathan is that God cannot be domesticated (just as Leviathan could not be). If these lessons are learned, coherence will be within reach. We can understand what our posture should be and how we should think about God and the world.

We have concluded that rest is the opposite of unrest, peace is the absence of fear and coherence is the opposite of confusion. The book of Job can help us find coherence through understanding, and it can help us find peace through trust. If our communities can rally around one who is suffering (as we are called to do) and if we can find the peace and rest that Christ offers in the kingdom of God, we can also find rest for our souls. Thus, the book moves beyond a superficial sense of comfort toward coherence, peace and rest that begin with trust and are ultimately fulfilled in Christ.

FOR FURTHER REFLECTION

1. Why is acceptance better than comfort?

2. How do we get rest in the midst of our burdens?

3. Explain the difference between rest and *shalom*.

4. How does Job help us find rest, peace and coherence and avoid unrest, fear and confusion?

TWENTY

APPLYING
THE BOOK OF JOB

We can now finally attempt to understand the application that should be made of the lessons that we learn from the book of Job. It is best to begin by making sure we understand what the application of biblical teaching should look like. It is important to draw a distinction between *remedial application* and *constructive application*. Remedial application is the form that application often takes in our churches today. Using this approach we come to recognize something we are doing wrong. This sort of application urges us to stop doing what we shouldn't be doing or to begin doing what we should be doing. In other words, after preaching on an Old Testament text, the preacher might urge the congregation to "go, thou, and do likewise!" or "go, thou, and don't do likewise!" Such application is sometimes referred to as the takeaway, and it often operates by instructing the hearers in steps that can be taken this week to begin to rectify the situation. The instruction may provide specific action points intended to correct harmful behaviors, adjust habits or restore relationships. Remedial application can be important and cannot be neglected, but it is only the beginning. We have to be engaged in doing more than correcting wrong behavior or thinking. That is where constructive application comes in.

Constructive application involves more than doing what is right; it puts us on a path of thinking what is right. It involves how we think about ourselves, about the world around us and, most importantly, about God. More than action points that can be undertaken this week, these thinking points provide the basis for a lifetime of inner resources that will help us respond well to situations that we may face tomorrow, next month or twenty years down the road.

Remedial application confronts our failures and inadequacies. Constructive application fills our reservoirs of understanding so we have something to draw on throughout life. Remedial application is like paying the outstanding bills in a financial crisis. Constructive application is like contributing to a savings account so financial crisis in the future can be avoided. The former perpetuates living hand to mouth; the latter builds financial security. Ideally, our spiritual lives should grow toward maturity by being securely anchored, fed by the deep reservoir of knowledge of God that his Word supplies. We do not want to be people who only survive hand to mouth spiritually. So when we look to Job for application, we should turn our attention to the long-term constructive application it offers, which can shape beliefs for a lifetime.

HOW WE SHOULD THINK ABOUT GOD

We saw that even before Job's disasters, he showed signs of thinking God was petty. Why else would he offer sacrifices for his children "just in case"? (See Job 1:4-5.) Once his suffering began he stated that opinion explicitly. One application of the book of Job is that we should learn not to make the mistake of thinking of God in that way. It is true that God knows everything about us—not only all that we have ever done but also our deepest thoughts and motivations. It is chilling when we ponder that fact, and though it can motivate us to purity, we cannot allow it to drive us to paranoia. Instead of thinking of it in Orwellian "big brother" terms (also a popular theme in modern entertainment), we should understand it in the light of grace.

Every sin is an offense against God, and he does hold us accountable. But he does not look for every minor infraction and then charge in with blows of major judgment. It should be noted that God was quite proud of Job and labeled him righteous, though we know well that no one is fully righteous. God is not picayune; God's judgments are not extreme beyond what has been earned. We also must remember that God in Christ has done all that is necessary to pay for our sins.

We know that God, like a good parent, disciplines those whom he loves. After all, the author of Hebrews tells us that God disciplines us like a father disciplines his son (Heb 12:4-13). But as we have learned in the book of Job, we must not be too quick to conclude that when things go wrong in our lives, God is disciplining us. Discipline is not very instructive or effective if sufferers do not know why they are being disciplined. As parents, we would not make such a mistake, so we should not think that God would be so opaque in discipline.

The point is that God is not accountable to us, and we should not be always standing ready to put him under the microscope for our approval. We should not harbor suspicions against God such that we are ready to doubt him and think the worst of him. As we have contended before, God should get the benefit of the doubt. Rather than believing that we could run the world better, we should recognize his grace as he is patient with our shortcomings and know that we can trust him because he loves us.

The biblical view of God, despite the presence of narratives throughout the Bible that may appear to suggest differently, is that God is consistent rather than arbitrary, good rather than evil and characterized by displays of grace rather than by uncontrolled power. God is not a chaos creature who is powerful, mischievous, arbitrary, amoral and driven by instincts and selfishness. That is not the God of the Bible. If we think we see evidence to the contrary, we ought to look again and think more deeply.

We have no place to gain a confident picture of God except from the Bible. Whatever we get from human speculation is just that. If this is so, we should be committed to the picture the Bible provides—the whole picture. Sometimes when we install new software on our computers we might be asked whether we want to do a full install or a custom install. Most of us don't know enough to do a custom install because we don't know what is important and what is not. Likewise, as the Bible gives us a picture of God, we cannot settle for a custom install. If we choose what we like and what we don't, we are merely shaping God in our own image.

We do not have that choice. We need the full install. That is what we mean when we talk about submitting to the Bible's authority.

In summary,

- God is not petty; he is a God of grace who knows our frailty and has arranged for our sins to be addressed. He disciplines in love and punishes guided by wisdom.

- God is not a chaos creature; his actions are perfectly in accord with his plans. Goodness, justice and wisdom flow from him and are characteristic of him. He is all-powerful but does not abuse his power as humans are inclined to do.

- We cannot do a better job than God; he cannot be charged with incompetence. We dare not think that we could focus on one issue (whether the suffering of a loved one or the starving children of the world) and think that if we could just fix that, somehow everything else could be adjusted.

The lessons of the book of Job are expressed well in Paul's benediction in Romans 11:33-35:

> Oh, the depth of the riches of the wisdom and knowledge of God!
>   How unsearchable his judgments,
>   and his paths beyond tracing out!
> "Who has known the mind of the Lord?
>   Or who has been his counselor?"
> "Who has ever given to God,
>   that God should repay them?"

Here we find affirmation of God's wisdom, which is unfathomable—precisely the position that Job came to at the end of the book (Job 42:1-6). Paul also acknowledges that God's judgments (i.e., the explanations of justice behind his actions) are beyond our ability to scrutinize and evaluate. Furthermore, we cannot know all that is in God's mind or all the details that he takes into account. When we recognize that we cannot give him counsel, we must conclude that whatever we may think, we are not better equipped to run the cosmos. Paul then concludes by reminding us that God owes us nothing. He does not need to compensate us for our righteousness. He has given all by giving his Son, and that is sufficient.

THINKING POINTS ABOUT GOD

Manipulating God. We saw that in the book of Job the friends advised Job to pursue a path of appeasement so that he could return to favor with God. Job refused that course of action, but he tried to manipulate God through his oath of innocence. It is a natural human instinct to want to affect God in some way so that he responds the way that we want him to. This inclination fit neatly into the ancient Near Eastern great-symbiosis thinking because the ancients believed that the gods had needs. Beings who have needs can be leveraged to do what you want.

In Israelite thinking, God does not have needs, but attempts are still made to affect his decisions by holding his character and reputation hostage. Any time that we try to get God to bend to our desires or requests, we are demonstrating a lack of respect for his wisdom. God does not have needs. Our gifts do not appease him or bribe him to act. Our praise does not flatter him and so cajole him into action on our behalf. We cannot use his character and reputation against him because he can only be who he is. No extortion or blackmail is possible, and we degrade God by approaching him on such terms.

We therefore need to be careful how and what we pray lest we slip into manipulative ways of thinking. We dare not try to change God; he needs to change us. Any picture of God we devise that allows us to coerce him into addressing our desires is bound to diminish him in the end. A god at our beck and call is no God. We should never think that we can back God into a corner by throwing his promises at him (likely not intended as promises anyway). We should never think that we can demand that God answer us as we specify and by our timetable. We should never think that because we consider ourselves faithful that God therefore owes us the sort of response that we desire. We can feel free to pray for those outcomes that we want (healing, guidance, etc.), but in his response God must be free to be God. Sometimes we need his strength to live with physical problems rather than his healing from those problems. Sometimes we need his encouragement to continue in what seems to us an untenable situation rather than persuading him to change our circumstances. In most cases, we are the ones who need to change: "your kingdom come [not mine]" (Lk 11:2); "your will be done [not mine]" (Mt 26:42). We should ponder the sort of people we should be in the circumstances in which we find ourselves. The prayers God most delights in answering are those that ask him to shape us into people who can serve and honor him where he places us.

Vindicating ourselves at God's expense. We always want to look good. *Proud* describes people who have an inordinately high opinion of themselves and think about themselves constantly; *vain* describes people who unjustifiably think that other people have a high opinion of them and think about them constantly. Pride can lead us to think that we deserve better than we are getting at God's hands. Vanity leads us to think that God should be more considerate of us—after all, we are important! In contrast to those who are prideful are those who suffer from low self-esteem. Those of us who struggle with this problem might believe that God should treat us more gently—after all, we are fragile! Any path of thinking that results in us being the winner and God being the loser is flawed.

All these inclinations bring us back to the idea that behind any attempt to vindicate ourselves is the idea of disappointment with God. We feel let down by what we experience, and we want to use some kind of persuasion to bring him around to our way of thinking. This is dangerous. From the Garden of Eden, the human plight has been characterized by our desire to "be like God" in all the wrong ways. From the start we wanted to be the center of order in our lives—born to be control freaks. We would like God to sing to our tune rather than fitting into what he is doing. When we vindicate ourselves at his expense, we are setting ourselves in his place.

Disinterested righteousness. Here we finally return to the issue that opens the book of Job and drives it. Is there such a thing as disinterested righteousness? Does anyone serve God for nothing? As we have noted, Job demonstrated that there was such a thing as disinterested righteousness, and he was an example of it. In the rhetorical strategy of the book, this means that God's policy of blessing righteous people has been successfully defended because it did not simply turn Job into a mercenary of sorts, serving God for the benefits he received. In the application of the book, we need to take the step of moving from the issue of God's policies and the question of whether Job served God for nothing to the question of whether we serve God for nothing. Is our righteousness and faithfulness disinterested?

We can get a better look at this by comparing Job's situation to Abraham's in Genesis 22 because they both focus on the same issue. When Abraham is asked to sacrifice Isaac, much more is at stake than the life of his beloved son. When Abraham puts Isaac on the altar, the covenant is on the altar. Without Isaac there will be no family and therefore no land and no blessing. The covenant in its entirety with all of its benefits will be forfeit if Isaac is sacrificed.

When we read Genesis 22 we often wonder why God would make such a request. Hadn't Abraham already demonstrated his faith over and over again? Indeed he had, but the text indicates that something else was at stake. The question is not whether Abraham has faith (in Gen 15:6 his faith had been affirmed) but whether he fears God (Gen 22:12). Why would that be in question? What is the alternative? When we approach the text with these questions, we see that, just as in the book of Job, what is being examined is Abraham's motivation for following God. Does Abraham serve God for nothing? All of Abraham's other manifestations of faith were in situations where he stood to gain something from God. He was asked to leave his land, but a better land was promised. He was asked to leave his family, but he was promised a large family of his own. He may have left his inheritance and status in the family behind, but he was promised manifold blessings.

By asking Abraham to sacrifice Isaac, God was seeking demonstration (not just cognitive knowledge) that Abraham's faith was motivated by fear of the Lord, not just by covenant benefits. Abraham's actions affirmed that he feared God and that he did so not only because so many benefits could be gained (Gen 22:15-18). He was not motivated by the great promises of God but by God himself, who was worthy to be feared.

When we look at Job and Abraham, we get a sense of what delights the heart of God. He has much to offer us as his people, and he delights in bringing blessing into our lives. He is honored by our praise and faithful lives. But he is most honored when our response to him is pure—not dependent on what we get out of it.

If we want to think about our lives in light of what we learn from Abraham and Job, we would have to pose the question this way: What if we lost all evidence of the blessing of God in our lives today (like Job did), and had no hope of future blessings (heaven, eternal life, etc.—the situation Abraham had to contemplate)? Would we still remain faithful to God and serve him with our lives? Do we serve God because he is worthy or because he is generous? Would we serve him if we had no benefits offered to us? Is our righteousness disinterested?

It is an important question to ask because it is easy to get careless. With eternal life in our pockets it is easy to forget that we are not on a ride with a prize at the end; we are in a relationship that carries responsibilities. Our relationship with God through Christ is not just about being saved *from* our sins; more importantly it is about being saved *to* a relationship with God. That relationship is not on hold until heaven. Being "in Christ" is more important than being "heaven bound." As the songwriter Andraé Crouch put it,

> But if heaven never was promised to me . . .
>   It's been worth just having the Lord in my life.

This perspective is difficult under any circumstances (since we can never really know for sure how we would respond), but it is most difficult when our circumstances are desperate and we feel hopeless. But this is precisely where the book of Job wants to put us. Do we stand ready to give an answer? This is exactly what Peter is talking about in 1 Peter 3:15: "But in your hearts revere Christ as Lord. Always be prepared to give an answer to everyone who asks you to give the reason for the hope that you have."

We often use this verse to talk about apologetics—that is, in giving an answer for our faith and hope. But notice that in this context Peter is talking about suffering; specifically, then, he exhorts us to be ready to give an answer for the hope that we have—*when we are suffering!* This is hope that will be impressive to the world around us—that we know how to respond when life falls apart. Then above all other times we should be committed to "revere Christ as Lord." Let us strive to be people who would serve God for nothing, people who are gratefully in relationship with God because he is worthy.

The constructive application from the book of Job then can be summarized as follows:

- Refrain from all attempts to manipulate God, because when we think about God that way, we diminish him. We must adopt a view of God that respects his wisdom.

- If we seek to elevate ourselves higher than God, we will end up with a God not worthy of our worship.

- We should strive to have a righteousness that is not based on the benefits we receive but is founded in the worthiness of God.

FOR FURTHER REFLECTION

1. How has your study of the book of Job changed your thinking, and how will it change your attitudes?

COMMENTARIES ON
THE BOOK OF JOB

For detailed expositions of the book of Job, we recommend the following two commentaries (not surprisingly). In these two commentaries a student can see how the perspective presented in this book plays out in the interpretation of the whole book of Job.

Longman, Tremper, III. *Job*. Baker Commentary on the Old Testament Wisdom and Psalms. Grand Rapids: Baker Academic, 2012.

Walton, John H. *Job*. NIV Application Commentary. Grand Rapids: Zondervan, 2012.

For those who want yet other perspectives, we recommend the following:

Andersen, Francis I. *Job*. Tyndale Old Testament Commentaries. Downers Grove, IL: InterVarsity Press, 2008. This is one of the best conservative commentaries on the book. It is limited by the length restrictions of the series but still extremely valuable as a lay commentary.

Clines, David J. A. *Job 1–20*, *Job 21–37* and *Job 38–42*. Word Biblical Commentary 17, 18A and 18B. Dallas/Nashville: Word/Thomas Nelson, 1989, 2006 and 2011. Clines has written a stimulating and insightful commentary on the book of Job—stimulating in the sense that it will get the reader thinking about the book and its issues. It is provocatively written. It is strong in literary and theological analysis and quite long because he extensively discusses linguistic, philological and textual issues. The bibliographies are incredibly good.

Habel, Norman C. *The Book of Job: A Commentary.* Old Testament Library. Philadelphia: Westminster, 1985. Habel has produced a major critical commentary on the book of Job. It is a fairly well-rounded commentary, but it concentrates particularly on literary features and theology. While Habel is aware of the questions surrounding the unity of Job, he treats it as a finished whole.

Hartley, John E. *The Book of Job.* New International Commentary on the Old Testament. Grand Rapids: Eerdmans, 1988. This is one of the most recent commentaries on Job. It is a major contribution to the study of the book, not necessarily because it is terribly original but because it examines all the facets of the book. It is solidly evangelical in its approach and very well researched.

Janzen, J. Gerald. *Job.* Interpretation. Atlanta: John Knox, 1990. In keeping with the parameters of the series, Janzen concentrates on theological significance and contemporary relevance. He does his job admirably, basing his work on an appraisal of such works as Pope and Gordis but often presenting new ideas. He makes a small yet significant shift away from the question, Why do the innocent suffer? to Why are the righteous pious? Very helpful and stimulating.

Seow, C.-L. *Job 1–21: Intrepretation and Commentary.* Illumination. Grand Rapids: Eerdmans, 2013. The first volume of Seow's commentary includes a rather extensive introduction that is particularly strong on the history of interpretation. He skillfully brings his abilities as an expert in ancient Near Eastern studies and the literature and theology of the Old Testament to bear on his interpretation of the text. The commentary divides its discussion of the text into two parts: the interpretation section, which is accessible to a wide reading public, and the commentary section, which contains more technical discussions of philology, text criticism and the like.

Chapter 2: What Is the Rhetorical Strategy of the Book of Job?

[1]The dialogues and discourses differ in that dialogues feature conversational exchanges between the parties whereas discourses resemble soliloquies or lectures.

[2]Widely accepted and nicely presented is Francis I. Andersen, *Job*, Tyndale Old Testament Commentaries (Downers Grove, IL: InterVarsity Press, 1976), pp. 222-24. Cf. J. F. A. Sawyer, "The Authorship and Structure of the Book of Job," in *Studia Biblica 1978*, ed. E. A. Livingstone, Journal for the Study of the Old Testament, Supplement Series 11 (Sheffield: University of Sheffield, 1979), pp. 253-57. For technical presentation see Michael Cheney, *Dust, Wind and Agony: Character, Speech and Genre in Job*, Coniectanea Biblica Old Testament 36 (Lund: Almqvist & Wiksell, 1994), pp. 42-45.

[3]Though if Job 28 is part of Job's speech, it may be seen as a temporary insight into the wisdom of God, an insight that soon gives way to anxiety and doubt. For this psychological interpretation of the placement of Job 28, see Tremper Longman III, *Job*, Baker Commentary on the Old Testament Wisdom and Psalms (Grand Rapids: Baker Academic, 2012), p. 61, citing Alison Lo, *Job 28 as Rhetoric: An Analysis of Job 28 in the Context of Job 22–31*, Supplement to Vetus Testamentum 97 (Leiden: Brill, 2003).

[4]John H. Walton, *Job*, NIV Application Commentary (Grand Rapids: Zondervan, 2012), pp. 30-31.

[5]Devised by Matitiahu Tsevat, "The Meaning of the Book of Job," *Hebrew Union College Annual* 37 (1966): 73-106.

Chapter 3: Job in the Context of the Ancient Near East

[1]This chapter was adapted from John H. Walton, *Job*, NIV Application Commentary (Grand Rapids: Zondervan, 2012), pp. 31-38.

²Dozens of articles could be cited, but the most informative are R. G. Albertson, "Job and Ancient Near Eastern Wisdom Literature," in *Scripture in Context II*, ed. William W. Hallo, J. C. Moyer and L. G. Perdue (Winona Lake, IN: Eisenbrauns, 1983), pp. 213-30; Daniel P. Bricker, "Innocent Suffering in Mesopotamia," *Tyndale Bulletin* 51 (2000): 121-42; J. E. Hartley, "Job 2: Ancient Near Eastern Background," in *Dictionary of the Old Testament: Wisdom, Poetry and Writings*, ed. Tremper Longman III and Peter Enns (Downers Grove, IL: InterVarsity Press, 2008), pp. 346-61; Gerald L. Mattingly, "The Pious Sufferer: Mesopotamia's Traditional Theodicy and Job's Counselors," in *The Bible in the Light of Cuneiform Literature: Scripture in Context III*, ed. William W. Hallo, Bruce William Jones and Gerald L. Mattingly (Lewiston, NY: Mellen Press, 1990), pp. 305-48; and Moshe Weinfeld, "Job and Its Mesopotamian Parallels—A Typological Analysis," in *Text and Context: Old Testament and Semitic Studies for F. C. Fensham*, ed. Walter T. Claassen, Journal for the Study of the Old Testament: Supplement 48 (Sheffield: JSOT Press, 1988), pp. 217-26.

³"Prayer to Every God," in *Ancient Near Eastern Texts Relating to the Old Testament*, ed. J. B. Pritchard, 3rd ed. (Princeton, NJ: Princeton University Press, 1969), pp. 391-92.

⁴Notice that in Job Yahweh removes his protection, allowing Job to be vulnerable to attack. Even so God identifies himself as the one who has been incited to ruin Job without cause (Job 2:3-6).

⁵Wilfred G. Lambert, *Babylonian Wisdom Literature* (Oxford: Clarendon Press, 1960): "Ludlul bēl Nēmeqi," 41:33-38.

Chapter 4: Is Job a Real Person?

¹Tremper Longman notes that Maimonides is one example of rabbinic interpreters who considered the book of Job to be a parable. Tremper Longman III, *Job*, Baker Commentary on the Old Testament Wisdom and Psalms (Grand Rapids: Baker Academic, 2012), p. 43.

²Cf. Moshe Greenberg, "Reflections on Job's Theology," in *Studies in the Bible and Jewish Thought* (Philadelphia: Jewish Publication Society, 1995), pp. 327-33, especially p. 328.

³Compare the allegory of the cave in Plato's *Republic* (7.514a-20a). Plato/Socrates is making a point about knowledge, not relating a narrative about some people who were in a cave. Likewise, Job is making a point about God's policies, not about some characters who had a conversation in heaven.

⁴There is some dispute over whether this Daniel is the Jewish exile who was

a contemporary of Ezekiel or a well-known worthy known from Ugaritic literature. See the debate between Harold H. P. Dressler, "The Identification of the Ugaritic *Dnil* with the Daniel of Ezekiel," *Vetus Testamentum* 29 (1979): 152-61, and John Day, "The Daniel of Ugarit and Ezekiel and the Hero of the Book of Daniel," *Vetus Testamentum* 30 (1980): 174-84.

[5]Likewise, there is little evidence to demonstrate that they *are* historical. Nevertheless, there is no demonstrably fictional character in ancient Near Eastern literature.

[6]Fictional characters such as Jason Bourne, James Bond and Indiana Jones have no known precedent in ancient literature.

[7]See the treatment by Wilfred G. Lambert, *Babylonian Wisdom Literature* (Oxford: Clarendon Press, 1960), p. 21.

[8]He shows that when the name comes first ("X is his name") rather than following ("His name was called X"), it is clear that everyone will recognize the name rather than that a character is being introduced for the first time. Meir Weiss, *The Story of Job's Beginning: Job 1–2; A Literary Analysis* (Jerusalem: Magnes, 1983), pp. 19-21.

[9]Note Weiss's indication of the consensus: "Scholars agree that the narrator did not invent Job" (ibid., p. 16).

[10]Thought experiments can be used in many of the sciences. In both philosophy and science, hypothetical situations are explored for their philosophical value. The point is not to claim that the events in the thought experiment did happen; instead they draw their philosophical strength from the realistic nature of the imaginative device. For explanation and example, see *Stanford Encyclopedia of Philosophy* (2014), ed. Edward N. Zalta, s.v. "Thought Experiments," by James Robert Brown and Yiftach Fehige, http://plato.stanford.edu/entries/thought-experiment. For discussion of thought experiments in science and also the belief that Job may be one, see William P. Brown, *The Seven Pillars of Creation: The Bible, Science, and the Ecology of Wonder* (Oxford: Oxford University Press, 2010), p. 115.

[11]For lengthy discussion, see Michael Cheney, *Dust, Wind and Agony: Character, Speech and Genre in Job*, Coniectanea Biblica Old Testament 36 (Lund: Almqvist & Wiksell, 1994), pp. 42-45.

Chapter 5: What Do We Learn About God from the Book of Job?

[1]Some have considered the book to be suitable for a dramatic performance,

and while that is not objectionable in any major way, it may not reflect the genre of the literature.

[2]Just as we are not claiming that the book is a drama, we are not claiming that it is a parable, but it shares some features with each of those genres.

Chapter 6: Who Is "Satan" in Job?

[1]Much of this chapter is drawn from John H. Walton, "Satan," in *Dictionary of the Old Testament: Wisdom, Poetry and Writings* (Downers Grove, IL: Inter-Varsity Press, 2008), pp. 214-17.

[2]See detailed discussion in John H. Walton, "Demons in Mesopotamia and Israel: Exploring the Category of Non-Divine but Supernatural Entities," in *Windows to the Ancient World of the Hebrew Bible: Essays in Honor of Samuel Greengus*, ed. Bill T. Arnold, Nancy L. Erickson and John H. Walton (Winona Lake, IN: Eisenbrauns, 2014), pp. 229-46.

[3]For a discussion of whether 1 Chronicles 21:1 evidences the word as a proper name or an indefinite accuser, see Sara Japhet, *I & II Chronicles: A Commentary*, Old Testament Library (Louisville, KY: Westminster John Knox, 1993), pp. 374-75. Peggy Lynne Day, *An Adversary in Heaven: Śāṭān in the Hebrew Bible*, Harvard Semitic Monographs 43 (Atlanta: Scholars Press, 1988), pp. 128-29, has suggested that the shift to using *Satan* as a proper name does not occur until the second century B.C. The earliest datable evidence for *satan* used as a proper name comes from *Jubilees* 23:29 and *Assumption of Moses* 10:1, both of which can be dated to the persecutions of Antiochus IV ca. 168 B.C. The deuterocanonical texts that antedate 168 B.C. speak of evil demons and corrupt angels, but no text uses the name *Satan*. In Tobit, for instance, the evil demon that had to be restrained before Tobit could marry Sarah is named Asmodeus (Tobit 3:8, 17). In the earliest level of *1 Enoch* 6–11, the leader of the angels who were punished as a consequence of their intercourse with the daughters of men is Shemihazah; in a later addition to these chapters, he is called Asael. In short, whereas the deuterocanonical literature prior to 168 B.C. speaks of specific names for evil demons and corrupt angels, no extant tradition employs the proper name *Satan*.

[4]Meir Weiss, *The Story of Job's Beginning: Job 1–2; A Literary Analysis* (Jerusalem: Magnes, 1983), pp. 35-41.

[5]There is a list of five *satan*s in *1 Enoch* 69:4-12, first century B.C. at the ear-

liest; see David S. Russell, *The Method and Message of Jewish Apocalyptic: 200 B.C.–A.D. 100*, Old Testament Library (Philadelphia: Westminster, 1964), pp. 254-55.

[6]E. Theodore Mullen Jr., *The Assembly of the Gods: The Divine Council in Canaanite and Early Hebrew Literature*, Harvard Semitic Monographs 24 (Chico, CA: Scholars Press, 1980), pp. 190-244; Weiss, *Story of Job's Beginning*, pp. 31-33.

[7]Day, *Adversary in Heaven*, pp. 80-81.

[8]*Dictionary of Deities and Demons in the Bible*, ed. Karel van der Toorn, Bob Becking and Pieter W. van der Horst, 2nd ed. (Grand Rapids: Eerdmans, 1999), p. 728.

[9]Implied in Job 1:12 and 2:3; Weiss, *Story of Job's Beginning*, p. 37.

[10]Weiss, *Story of Job's Beginning*, p. 37.

[11]Ibid., pp. 36-37; see also Carol L. Meyers and Eric M. Meyers, *Haggai, Zechariah 1–8*, Anchor Bible (Garden City, NY: Doubleday, 1987), pp. 185-86.

[12]Weiss, *Story of Job's Beginning*, p. 37.

[13]Meyers and Meyers, *Haggai, Zechariah 1–8*, p. 186.

[14]Day, *Adversary in Heaven*, pp. 118-21.

[15]Russell, *Method and Message of Jewish Apocalyptic*, p. 189.

Chapter 7: What Is the Role of Job in the Book of Job?

[1]Tremper Longman III, *Job,* Baker Commentary on the Old Testament Wisdom and Prophets (Grand Rapids: Baker Academic, 2012), p. 75.

[2]The research on the preposition was prompted by in-class questions asked by my (John's) student Jameson Ross.

Chapter 8: How to Assess Job's Human Advisers

[1]Drawn from John H. Walton, *Job*, NIV Application Commentary (Grand Rapids: Zondervan, 2012), pp. 182-84, 223-25 and 264-65.

Chapter 9: Who Is Job's Advocate?

[1]For full discussion of the options, see John B. Curtis, "On Job's Witness in Heaven," *JBL* 102 (1983): 549-62; F. Rachel Magdalene, "Who Is Job's Redeemer? Job 19:25 in Light of Neo-Babylonian Law," *Zeitschrift für Altorientalische und Biblische Rechtsgeschichte* 10 (2004): 292-316.

[2]Note how in Genesis 4:10 the blood of Abel cries out for vengeance and justice to be done.

[3]It occurs in the Sefire inscriptions, Ahiqar and the Dead Sea Scrolls as well as in Laban's Aramaic name for the pile of stones that stood as witness between him and Jacob (*Jegar Sahadutha*, Gen 31:47).

[4]David J. A. Clines, *Job 1–20*, Word Biblical Commentary (Dallas: Word, 1989), pp. 389-90, 459; accepted tentatively by Gerald H. Wilson, *Job*, New International Biblical Commentary (Peabody, MA: Hendrickson, 2007), p. 377.

[5]John E. Hartley, *The Book of Job*, New International Commentary on the Old Testament (Grand Rapids: Eerdmans, 1988); Edouard Dhorme, *A Commentary on the Book of Job*, trans. Harold Knight (repr., Nashville: Nelson, 1984); Robert Gordis, *The Book of Job: Commentary, New Translation and Special Studies*, Moreshet 2 (New York: JTS Press, 1978); H. H. Rowley, *The Book of Job*, New Century Bible (Grand Rapids: Eerdmans, 1981); Francis I. Andersen, *Job*, Tyndale Old Testament Commentaries (Nottingham: InterVarsity Press, 1976); and Samuel R. Driver, *Job*, International Critical Commentary (1921; repr., New York: T & T Clark, 2000).

[6]Bruce K. Waltke, *The Book of Proverbs, Chapters 15–31*, New International Commentary on the Old Testament (Grand Rapids: Eerdmans, 2005), p. 97, extends the closeness of this sort of friend to include taking up the case of the oppressed person in court, the role that a "brother" (relative) should play.

[7]This is not a common view, but it is not unprecedented. Wilson, *Job*, p. 377, appears to accept it.

[8]Peggy Lynne Day, *An Adversary in Heaven: Śāṭān in the Hebrew Bible*, Harvard Semitic Monographs 43 (Atlanta: Scholars Press, 1988), pp. 89-90, an option supported by Norman C. Habel, *The Book of Job: A Commentary*, Old Testament Library (Philadelphia: Westminster, 1985); Marvin H. Pope, *Job*, 3rd ed., Anchor Bible 15 (Garden City, NY: Doubleday, 1973); and Elmer B. Smick, "Job," in *The Expositor's Bible Commentary*, ed. Frank E. Gaebelein (Grand Rapids: Zondervan, 1988), 4:843-1000; and cf. Robert S. Fyall, *Now My Eyes Have Seen You: Images of Creation and Evil in the Book of Job*, New Studies in Biblical Theology 12 (Downers Grove, IL: InterVarsity Press, 2002), p. 40. F. Rachel Magdalene, *On the Scales of Righteousness: Neo-Babylonian Trial Law and the Book of Job* (Providence, RI: Brown Judaic Studies, 2007), pp. 221-22, suggests that

the specified role is "second accuser"—someone to stand alongside Job and second his accusation.

[9]For those who would like to see the technical support, see John H. Walton, *Job*, NIV Application Commentary (Grand Rapids: Zondervan, 2012), pp. 450-53.

[10]For more, see chap. 17 (part 4: Reading Job as a Christian).

Chapter 10: Behemoth and Leviathan, the Most Powerful Creatures Imaginable

[1]John Day, *God's Conflict with the Dragon and the Sea: Echoes of a Canaanite Myth in the Old Testament* (Cambridge: Cambridge University Press, 1985), gives an extensive list of other differences between crocodiles and Leviathan (pp. 65-66) and differences between hippopotami and Behemoth (pp. 76-77).

[2]R. Clifford, *Creation Accounts in the Ancient Near East and the Bible*, Catholic Biblical Quarterly Monograph Series 26 (Washington, DC: Catholic Biblical Association, 1994), pp. 194-95. See M. Wakeman, *God's Battle with the Monster: Study in Biblical Imagery* (Leiden: Brill, 1973). Robert S. Fyall, *Now My Eyes Have Seen You: Images of Creation and Evil in the Book of Job*, New Studies in Biblical Theology 12 (Downers Grove, IL: InterVarsity Press, 2002), pp. 126-37, accepts the connection of Behemoth with Mot but considers Leviathan to be best identified with Satan.

[3]Day, *God's Conflict*, pp. 72-81.

[4]In this interpretation, "Terrors" in Job 30:15 and "Night" in Job 30:17 are seen as personifications (with grammatical support). To the extent that this is so, God has joined these chaos elements in oppressing Job. For more discussion, see John H. Walton, *Job*, NIV Application Commentary (Grand Rapids: Zondervan, 2012), p. 317.

[5]Samuel E. Balentine, "'What Are Human Beings, That You Make So Much of Them?': Divine Disclosure from the Whirlwind: 'Look at Behemoth,'" in *God in the Fray: A Tribute to Walter Brueggemann*, ed. Tod Linafelt and Timothy K. Beal (Minneapolis: Fortress, 1998), pp. 259-78, especially pp. 270-71; and John G. Gammie, "Behemoth and Leviathan: On the Didactic and Theological Significance of Job 40:15–41:26," in *Israelite Wisdom: Theological and Literary Essays in Honor of Samuel Terrien*, ed. John G. Gammie, Walter A. Brueggemann, W. Lee Humphreys and James M. Ward (Missoula, MT: Scholars Press, 1978), pp. 217-31, especially pp. 221-22.

[6]Norman C. Habel, *The Book of Job: A Commentary*, Old Testament Library (Philadelphia: Westminster, 1985), pp. 570-71, picks up a piece of this in his comment: "Now Yahweh challenges Job to consider how he could possibly take his stand before God's 'face' if he cannot survive a confrontation with Leviathan." But he does not follow that observation to the conclusions reached here. Likewise, Carol A. Newsome, *The Book of Job: A Contest of Moral Imaginations* (Oxford: Oxford University Press, 2003), p. 252, also perceives the comparison as she speaks of a "curious level of identification between God and Leviathan" but fails to follow this thought to its logical conclusion.

[7]This paragraph and the following bullet points are taken from Walton, *Job*, pp. 408-9.

[8]This is a unique collocation. Usually when the verb *'asah* is used with the preposition *'im*, there is also an adjective (X) or longer descriptions of behavior, and the meaning is, e.g., "I have acted in X way toward you" (see other uses in Job 10:12; 13:20). Here there is no adjective, but the way God has acted toward Job could feasibly, though elliptically, be picked up in the opening reference to Behemoth: "Behold Behemoth, I have acted toward you [as if you were him]." Admittedly there are clearer ways that this could be said, but that would be true no matter how one interprets the verse.

[9]Day, *God's Conflict*, p. 69, says: "One may therefore reasonably conclude that the list of things connected with the subduing of Leviathan . . . , which are impossible for Job, represents what God has actually done. The message therefore presupposes a battle in which God defeated Leviathan." One can see that Day imposes all of this on the text, which says nothing about God battling Leviathan or defeating him.

[10]Fyall, *Now My Eyes Have Seen You*, p. 157.

Chapter 11: The Retribution Principle and Theodicy in Job

[1]Much of the information in this chapter was adapted from John H. Walton, "Retribution," in *Dictionary of the Old Testament: Wisdom, Poetry and Writings* (Downers Grove, IL: InterVarsity Press, 2008), pp. 647-55.

[2]Karel van der Toorn, "Theodicy in Akkadian Literature," in *Theodicy in the World of the Bible*, ed. Antti Laato and Johannes C. de Moor (Leiden: Brill, 2003), p. 62.

[3]Jan Assmann, *The Mind of Egypt: History and Meaning in the Time of the Pharaohs* (New York: Metropolitan Books, 2002), p. 128.

Chapter 12: The Retribution Principle in Wisdom Literature

[1]Raymond C. Van Leeuwen, "Wealth and Poverty: System and Contradiction in Proverbs," *Hebrew Studies* 33 (1992): 25-36. More recently, Tremper Longman III, *How to Read Proverbs* (Downers Grove, IL: InterVarsity Press, 2002), p. 89-90.

[2]See Bruce Waltke, "Does Proverbs Promise Too Much?," *Andrews University Seminary Studies* 34 (1996): 319-36.

[3]Van Leeuwen, "Wealth and Poverty."

Chapter 13: Does Job Believe in the Afterlife?

[1]We would have to reserve Egypt for a different discussion, but Egyptian views have no influence in the discussion of conceptual ideas in Job.

[2]For detailed discussion and defense of this translation, see John H. Walton, *Job*, NIV Application Commentary (Grand Rapids: Zondervan, 2012), pp. 178-79; and Tremper Longman III, *Job*, Baker Commentary on the Old Testament Wisdom and Psalms (Grand Rapids: Baker Academic, 2012), pp. 207-8. Part of the debate concerns whether to go with what is written in the text (the negative *lo'*) or with what the scribes propose to be read here (the asseverative *lu*).

[3]The word translated "renewal" in Job 14:14 refers to someone or something that replaces another. Job expects that his turn will come to have his case heard (Job 14:15-17).

[4]See extensive technical discussion in Walton, *Job*, pp. 219-21.

[5]For the most complete discussion and critique of etymological suggestions, see Theodore Lewis, "Dead, Abode of the," *Anchor Bible Dictionary*, ed. David Noel Freedman (New York: Doubleday, 1992), 2:101-2.

[6]Ruth Rosenberg contends that Sheol and the pit are places for the "wicked dead"—those who suffer untimely or unnatural death. She sees the alternative as being gathered to one's ancestors. "The Concept of Biblical Sheol Within the Context of Ancient Near Eastern Beliefs" (dissertation, Harvard, 1981), pp. 174-93. Nonetheless, her evidence is not able to rule out the idea that the untimely/unnatural death itself is the punishment of God, or that going down to the pit simply refers to improper burial. Additionally, verses like 1 Kings 2:6 suggest that one could go down to Sheol "in peace." Rosenberg's explanation of this passage ("Concept of Biblical Sheol," pp. 240-41) is unconvincing.

[7]Nicholas J. Tromp, *Primitive Conceptions of Death and the Nether World in the*

Old Testament (Rome: Pontifical Biblical Institute, 1969), pp. 187-90. Tromp has the most thorough treatment of Sheol and other netherworld concepts, though see more recently Philip Johnston, *Shades of Sheol: Death and Afterlife in the Old Testament* (Downers Grove, IL: InterVarsity Press, 2002).

[8]Tromp, *Primitive Conceptions,* pp. 190-94. This notwithstanding Rosenberg's etymological analysis. She offers a sound defense of *she'ol* as derived from the root š'l meaning "to conduct an investigation" (found with this meaning also in Ugaritic, Akkadian and Aramaic) and thus conveying a forensic concept of "call to account (= punish)" ("Concept of Biblical Sheol," pp. 9-12). Rosenberg does not succeed, however, in demonstrating that the etymology has carried over into the concepts attached to the meaning of the term in Israelite usage.

[9]Robert Martin-Achard, *From Death to Life: A Study of the Development of the Doctrine of the Resurrection in the Old Testament*, trans. John Penney Smith (Edinburgh: Oliver & Boyd, 1960), pp. 39-40. Though Enoch and Elijah are exceptional cases, we should note that the text does not indicate where they went in either instance. In Elijah's case he goes up to heaven (2 Kings 2:11), but "heaven" is also the word for sky in Hebrew; it is clear from the response of the other prophets (2 Kings 2:16) that they understand the word in that way (cf. Ezek 3:14-15; 8:3).

[10]The combination is used elsewhere in Leviticus 19:10 ("leave them"), Job 39:14 ("lets them"), Psalm 16:10 ("abandon me") and Malachi 4:1 ("be left to them") and in each case means "consign to." Even in Job 39:14, the ostrich does not "abandon" her eggs in the earth but consigns them to the earth, which helps to protect them.

[11]Most occurrences use the word as the nominalized object of prepositions. The four occurrences similar to Psalm 16 are in Jeremiah 15:18 (perpetual pain), Amos 1:11 (perpetual anger of Edom against Israel), Psalm 13:2 (the Lord's apparent perpetual neglect of the psalmist) and Psalm 74:3 (the perpetual state of ruin of Jerusalem).

[12]The feminine plural form occurs only here, but the masculine plural occurs in Psalm 16:6 and in Job 36:11.

[13]For further discussion of the important distinctions between message and fulfillment, see Andrew E. Hill and John H. Walton, *Survey of the Old Testament*, 3rd ed. (Grand Rapids: Zondervan, 2009), pp. 508-15.

[14]The NIV has correctly rendered the Hebrew term *nephesh* as "me" rather than "my soul"; in fact, there is no place in the Old Testament where *nephesh*

demonstrably refers to the soul in the theological sense. Rather *nephesh* refers to one's self or one's being.

[15]This is attested as early as the books of Enoch in the early second century. The Septuagint distinguishes between Hades and Gehenna, which in early church history were identified respectively as places of purgation and torment. Evidence for two compartments also occurs in the parable of Lazarus and the rich man (Lk 16).

[16]David S. Russell, *The Method and Message of Jewish Apocalyptic: 200 B.C.–A.D. 100*, Old Testament Library (Philadelphia: Westminster, 1964), pp. 357-66. For detailed treatment of various traditions concerning resurrection during the intertestamental period, see George W. E. Nickelsburg, *Resurrection, Immortality, and Eternal Life in Intertestamental Judaism*, Harvard Theological Studies 26 (Cambridge, MA: Harvard University Press, 1972).

Chapter 14: Learning About the Cosmos from the Book of Job

[1]Del Ratzsch, *Science & Its Limits: The Natural Sciences in Christian Perspective*, 2nd ed. (Downers Grove, IL: InterVarsity Press, 2000), especially pp. 26-27.

[2]The verse uses the same word as Genesis 1:2, *tohu*.

[3]Full discussion is available in John H. Walton, *Job*, NIV Application Commentary (Grand Rapids: Zondervan, 2012), pp. 251-54.

[4]Only in the new creation will the consummation of God's plan be reached as no non-order will remain (Rev 21:1, there will be no sea, etc.).

Chapter 15: The Theology of Suffering in the Book of Job

[1]Arthur J. Gossip, "But When Life Tumbles In, What Then?," sermon, Beechgrove Church, Aberdeen, Scotland, 1927.

[2]Terence E. Fretheim, *Creation Untamed: The Bible, God, and Natural Disasters* (Grand Rapids: Baker Academic, 2010), p. 109.

[3]John Polkinghorne, *Quarks, Chaos & Christianity: Questions to Science and Religion*, rev. ed. (New York: Crossroad, 2006), p. 61.

Chapter 16: Job's View of God

[1]It must be noted, however, that this is a more limited expectation than is normally recognized. Note the parallel passage in Luke 6:36: "Be merciful, just as your Father is merciful [*oiktirmon*]." The term in Matthew ("perfect")

is often used to refer to spiritual maturity; see 1 Corinthians 2:6 ("mature"); 14:20 ("adults"); Philippians 3:15 ("mature"); and Hebrews 5:14 ("mature"); 6:1("maturity"). The context in Luke is the Sermon on the Mount, and Jesus has just made several points in antithesis. As a conclusion to the last antithesis in the series, it might best be rendered, "Be non-discriminating as your father in heaven is non-discriminating."

Chapter 17: Job and Jesus

[1]Jon D. Levenson, *The Hebrew Bible, the Old Testament, and Historical Criticism: Jews and Christians in Biblical Studies* (Louisville: Westminster John Knox, 1993), p. 9.

[2]Walter C. Kaiser Jr., *The Messiah in the Old Testament*, Studies in Old Testament Biblical Theology (Grand Rapids: Zondervan, 1995), pp. 61-64.

[3]See Daniel Golman, *Emotional Intelligence: Why It Can Matter More Than IQ* (New York: Bantam, 2005).

[4]See Ben Witherington III, *Jesus the Sage: The Pilgrimage of Wisdom* (Minneapolis: Fortress, 1994).

[5]For full development, see Tremper Longman III, *Proverbs*, Baker Commentary on the Old Testament Wisdom and Psalms (Grand Rapids: Baker, 2006), pp. 58-61, 110-14, 194-213.

[6]"Righteousness," in The *Baker Illustrated Bible Dictionary*, ed. Tremper Longman III (Grand Rapids: Baker Books, 2013), p. 1429.

[7]Friedrich Delitzsch, *Biblical Commentary on the Book of Job* (repr., Grand Rapids: Eerdmans, 1970), p. 32.

Author Index

SUBJECT INDEX

Scripture Index